"BEHOLD THE MAN!"

Pilate condemned his own judgment with the words, "Take ye Him, and crucify Him: for I find no fault in Him." (Antonio Ciseri, Artist)

"BEHOLD THE MAN!"

A Review of the Trials
and Crucifixion of Jesus

The Biblical Record in the
Light of Hebrew and Roman Law

by

TAYLOR G BUNCH

SOUTHERN PUBLISHING ASSOCIATION

NASHVILLE 8, TENNESSEE

(Printed in U. S. A.)

CONTENTS

CHAPTER ONE

"BEHOLD THE MAN!"

"THEN came Jesus forth, wearing the crown of thorns, and the purple robe. And Pilate saith unto them, Behold the Man!" John 19: 5.

We cannot know the Roman governor's real estimate of Jesus further than that he believed Him to be innocent of all charges brought against Him by the Jews and that He was the victim of a cruel conspiracy. Pilate was doubtless well impressed with the Man of Galilee because of His noble conduct and godly bearing during the long trial that was now coming to a tragic end. When, a little later, the Jews demanded the death of Jesus because He claimed to be the Son of God, Pilate was frightened, and was more determined than ever to release Him. It is evident that the governor regarded Jesus as no ordinary man, and his final appeal was to the sympathy of the mob as he set Jesus forth before them and cried out, "Behold the Man!"

The history of mankind is chiefly the record of the character and exploits of the men and women who exerted the greatest influence upon their generation and nation. A nation's history is inseparably connected with the careers of the leading characters of its national life. They are the makers of history, the beacons of civilization. We cannot think of the empire of Babylon apart from Nebuchadnezzar, its greatest ruler and builder, and Daniel, its greatest statesman and prime minister. Cyrus, Darius Hystaspes, and Xerxes were the makers of Persian history; and Greece revolved around a small galaxy of her mighty men, including Socrates, Plato, and Alexander. Roman history was made by a few generals, scholars, and Cæsars; and the modern nations owe their existence and glory to a small group of their national heroes. The careers and influence of earth's mighty men, however, have been short-lived. Like shooting meteors they blazed amid the darkness for a few brief moments, and then burned out and disappeared in virtual oblivion.

The Man of Men

Just as national history and national heroes are inseparable, so world history can be rightly understood and appreciated only in the light of the deeds, character, and influence of Jesus Christ. He is the man of men, the hero of heroes, the beacon of all history, the great I AM of all time. He is the "Son of man," indicating that He belongs to all mankind in every age. He is the arbiter of individual and world destiny. True history is really "His story." Jesus Christ is the creator, preserver, benefactor, and redeemer of all mankind. He is "the first and the last" in all that is worth while; He is the "Alpha and Omega" of all that is to be desired. He is the author of all light and truth, and the finisher of all righteousness.

Though written by more than forty men, covering a period of fifteen centuries, the Bible is the only history that gives the proper place in its records to the Creator and Ruler who presides "over the kings of the earth;" who "ruleth in the kingdom of men, and giveth it to whomsoever He will." Revelation 17: 18; Daniel 4: 32. One of the greatest of earthly rulers, after a humiliating experience in which he learned the true principles of sovereignty, said: "At the end of the days I Nebuchadnezzar lifted up mine eyes to heaven, and mine understanding returned unto me, and I blessed the Most High, and I praised and honored Him that liveth forever, whose dominion is an everlasting dominion, and His kingdom is from generation to generation: and all the inhabitants of the earth are reputed as nothing: and He doeth according to His will in the army of heaven, and among the inhabitants of the earth: and none can stay His hand, or say unto Him, What doest Thou?" Daniel 4: 34, 35.

The Scriptures were written, not so much to record the history of the past, or to forecast the events of the future, or to enunciate a system of theology, although they do all this, but to reveal to the human family a Person. The Bible is not so much a book of theology as it is a biography of its author and chief subject, Jesus Christ. The Bible deals with the various sciences, so that scientists, while searching for light in their particular fields, might discover the science of salvation. It deals briefly with geology, that men interested in that subject may be led to discover the Rock of Ages. The Scriptures contain a great deal of invaluable information regarding medical science, so that men who devote their lives to the science of healing might become acquainted with the Great Physician, who alone can heal the malady of sin and give eternal life. Astronomers may find much to inspire them in the Bible; but, best of all, it will lead to the discovery of "the Bright and Morning Star" and "the Sun of Righteousness." In the Holy Word botanists may find "the Lily of the valley" and "the Rose of Sharon," and zoologists will have revealed to them "the Lamb of God" and "the Lion of the tribe of Judah." The principal purpose of the Scriptures is to make known to man "the One altogether lovely," "the Chiefest among ten thousand."

From the viewpoint of His humanity alone, Jesus is the incomparable. "Jesus of Nazareth, our divinest symbol! Higher has the human thought not yet reached," said

Thomas Carlyle; and Johann Herder declared that "Jesus Christ is in the noblest, and most perfect sense, the realized ideal of humanity." Ernest Renan testifies that "the Christ of the Gospels is the most beautiful incarnation of God in the most beautiful of forms. His beauty is eternal; His reign will never end;" and Goethe said: "I esteem the Gospels to be thoroughly genuine, for there shines forth from them the reflected splendor of a sublimity, proceeding from the person of Jesus Christ, of so divine a kind as only the divine could ever have manifested upon earth."

"Will Jesus ever be surpassed?" asked the editor of the Los Angeles *Times*. He then answers: "Nineteen hundred years have passed, and His equal has not risen. This is not true of the world's other great ones. Every generation produces geniuses worthy to be compared with those who have gone before. It can be said of no one man, 'He stands alone; he has no rival; no equal; no superior.' But this is true of Jesus. Nineteen hundred years, instead of diminishing His greatness, have accentuated it. Today, more than ever before, the limelight is on the Nazarene."

One day as Napoleon Bonaparte was talking to his attendant in the place of his banishment on the island of St. Helena regarding the heroes of history, he suddenly turned and asked the question, "Can you tell me who Jesus Christ was?" As the officer hesitated, Napoleon said: "Well, then, I will tell you. I think I understand somewhat of human nature, and I tell you all these were men, and I am a man, but not one is like Him; Jesus Christ was more than man. Alexander, Cæsar, Charlemagne, and myself founded great empires; but upon what did the creations of our genius depend? Upon force. Jesus alone founded His empire upon love, and to this very day millions would die for Him. . . .

He asks for the human heart; He demands it unconditionally, and forthwith His demand is granted. Wonderful! All who sincerely believe in Him experience that remarkable supernatural love towards Him. Time, the great destroyer, is powerless to extinguish this sacred flame."

" 'The gospel is no mere book,' said he [Napoleon] at another time, 'but a living creature, with a vigor, a power, which conquers all that opposes it. Here lies the Book of books upon the table [touching it reverently]; I do not tire of reading it, and do so daily with equal pleasure. The soul, charmed with the beauty of the gospel, is no longer its own: God possesses it entirely: He directs its thoughts and faculties; it is His. What a proof of the divinity of Jesus Christ! Yet in this absolute sovereignty He has but one aim—the spiritual perfection of the individual, the purification of his conscience, his union with what is true, the salvation of his soul. Men wonder at the conquests of Alexander, but here is a conqueror who draws men to Himself for their highest good; who unites to Himself, incorporates into Himself, not a nation, but the whole human race!' "—"*Scripture of Truth,*" *Sidney Collett;* "*The Life and Words of Christ,*" *Cunningham Geikie, pages 2, 3.*

We shall close these testimonies of men regarding the character and mission of Christ with a statement made by William Jennings Bryan: "Reared in a carpenter shop, with no knowledge of literature save Bible literature, with no acquaintance with philosophers living or with the writings of sages dead, when only about thirty years old He gathered disciples about Him, promulgated a higher code of morals than the world had ever known before, and proclaimed Himself the Messiah. He taught and performed miracles for a few brief months and then was crucified; His disciples were scattered and many of them put to death; His claims were disputed, His resurrection denied, and His followers persecuted; and yet from this beginning His religion spread until hundreds of millions have taken His name with reverence upon their lips, and millions have been willing to die rather than surrender the faith which He put into their hearts. How shall we account for Him? Here is the greatest fact of history; here is One who has with increasing power, for nineteen hundred years, molded the hearts, the thoughts, and the lives of men, and He exerts more influence today than ever before."

The men quoted above are only a few of the many who today join in the exclamation, "Behold the Man!"

CHAPTER TWO

"BEHOLD THE LAMB OF GOD!"

SOME TIME after the baptism of Jesus, John the Baptist saw Him approaching, and said to his own disciples: "Behold the Lamb of God, which taketh away the sin of the world." The next day he again saw the Master walking, and, pointing to Him, said: "Behold the Lamb of God!" See John 1:29, 35, 36.

It is not sufficient that the human race behold Jesus as the Man of men, the Superman. He is not only the *Man* of God; He is also the *Lamb* of God. As Emmanuel, the God-man, Jesus Christ is the great Sin Bearer. Jesus is man's outstanding example, "the realized ideal of humanity;" but He is more than that: He is the Saviour and Redeemer of all who accept His grace and surrender to His sovereign will. As the Son of man and the Son of God, Christ saves from sin and all its terrible consequences. The repentant sinner need only fix his eyes upon the Lamb of God to be so completely transformed that his fear is turned to joy and his doubts to hope. The stony heart is broken under the compelling power of grace, and a tide of love sweeps over the soul. Beholding Jesus as the great atonement for sin is the secret of the transformation of character into the divine image.

Jesus said: "This is My Father's will, that everyone who fixes his gaze on the Son of God and believes in Him should have the Life of the Ages, and I will raise him to life on the last day." John 6:40, Weymouth. The power of a fixed gaze to reproduce what is looked upon is beautifully illustrated by the camera. In order to reproduce the likeness of a landscape or a person, the camera must be fixed in an im movable position till the image is formed on the delicate film. The eyes or lens must be focused on the object to be photographed, and the gaze must remain fixed until the light completes the impression. The film must then be taken to the darkroom and be submitted to a chemical bath in order to bring to view all the beautiful details of the reproduction.

Someone has said that "Christ is sitting for His portrait in every disciple." He is posing for the reproduction of His image in us, and the gaze must remain fixed till His character is fully reproduced. As in the photograph, the darkroom experience and the acid test of fiery trials are necessary in order to develop and to make visible what has been impressed upon the mind and heart by beholding Jesus. These were the experiences that developed into visibility the marvelous perfections of Christ's matchless character. The darkroom of obscurity and trial developed the character of Joseph in Egypt, of Moses in the wilderness, of David in exile from the wrath of Saul, of Daniel in Babylonian captivity, and of Paul during the severe persecutions that ended in his martyrdom. In Malachi 3: 3 Jesus is represented as a silversmith watching the metal in the fiery furnace until the dross is all burned away and He can see in the silver the reflection of His own image. It is a true saying that "fiery trials make golden Christians." Jesus always beholds those who behold Him.

"All who long to bear the likeness of the character of God shall be satisfied. The Holy Spirit never leaves unassisted the soul who is looking unto Jesus. . . . If the eye is kept fixed on Christ, the work of the Spirit ceases not until the soul is conformed to His image. The pure element of love will expand the soul, giving it a capacity for higher attainments, for increased knowledge of heavenly things, so that it will not rest short of the fullness."—"*The Desire of Ages,*" *E. G. White, page 302.*

Beholding the Man of God transfixes the gaze and produces admiration. Beholding the Lamb of God reaches the heart and effects a transformation.

THE TRANSFORMING POWER OF CHRIST

Of the transforming power of beholding, the apostle Paul wrote: "We all, with open face beholding as in a glass the glory of the Lord, are changed into the same image from glory to glory, even as by the Spirit of the Lord." 2 Corinthians 3:18. The glory and the image of God represent His character. By beholding the character of Christ we are changed into His image, or likeness. This transformation from one degree of holiness to another depends on the constancy with which we keep our eyes fixed upon the Master Pattern. The development of character by the beholding process is gradual; it is a growth. The character goal of spiritual growth is to develop "unto a perfect man, unto the measure of the stature of the fullness of Christ." Ephesians 4:13.

Our characters are determined by what we look at, whether it be through the physical eyes, or the mind—the eyes of the soul. We always look at what we think about, and we think about what we look at. "As he [a man] thinketh in his heart, so is he," is a well-known proverb. Proverbs 23:7. Looking at and thinking about the faults of others has an unconscious influence that will eventually place them in our own characters. On the other hand, to fix our thoughts on things that are true, honest, pure, lovely, virtuous, and praiseworthy will have a powerful influence in developing these beautiful traits of character in us. See Philippians 4:8. It is because all these desirable virtues are found only in

Christ that we are admonished to keep our eyes fixed upon Him. In Him are none of the character blotches and blemishes common to humanity, the beholding of which would warp and dwarf our own character development.

As the mind dwells upon the Lamb of God, the character is molded after the divine similitude. As we contemplate His matchless character, His love encloses us, and our thoughts are pervaded with a sense of His goodness and mercy. His image is imprinted upon the eye of the soul, and every portion of the daily life is affected by a power that softens and subdues the whole nature. The mysterious power of faith, adoration, and love will be awakened in the soul of him who constantly beholds the character of Christ through a study of the Scriptures. As the vision is fixed upon the character of the Holy One, the beholder grows into the likeness of the Man of Calvary whom he adores.

The author of the epistle to the Hebrews said: "Wherefore, holy brethren, partakers of the heavenly calling, consider the Apostle and High Priest of our profession, Christ Jesus." Hebrews 3:1. "Fix your thoughts on Jesus" and "Fix your attention on Jesus" are other translations. "Consider" means "to look at closely, to observe; to fix the mind on, with a view to careful examination; to think on with care; to ponder, to study, to meditate on, to view attentively; to take time to consider well." Never will a true follower of Christ cease to keep his mind and attention centered upon Him who is both the victim and the priest. A Christian is one who is Christlike. In order to be like Christ we must continually behold Him to see what He is like. He is also our guide, and we are to "walk even as He walked." A disciple is one who follows another. A guide, in order to be successfully followed, must always be kept in view.

"BEHOLD THE LAMB OF GOD!"

There are many different viewpoints from which we can consider Jesus; but beholding Him as the Lamb of God involves a contemplation of His atoning sacrifice and crucifixion. It therefore calls for a consideration of the closing scenes of His earthly sojourn, culminating in His death. It was at the cross that mercy and truth met together, that righteousness and peace kissed each other. It is the thought of Calvary that awakens tender and sacred emotions in the heart. Pride and self-sufficiency cannot flourish in the soul that keeps fresh in memory the trials, crucifixion, and death of the Lamb of God. The contemplation of these scenes will fill the mind, touch and melt the soul, and produce a complete transformation of character. The purpose of this book is to focus our attention on those scenes and events upon which depend our eternal destiny.

Eloquent Testimony

Before entering more directly into our subject, let us consider one more testimony concerning Him whose outstanding success was due to His character and His suffering: "This Jesus of Nazareth, without money and arms, conquered more millions than Alexander, Cæsar, Mohammed, and Napoleon; without science and learning, He shed more light on things human and divine than all philosophers and scholars combined; without the eloquence of schools, He spoke such words of life as were never spoken before or since, and produced effects which lie beyond the reach of orator or poet; without writing a single line, He set more pens in motion, and furnished themes for more sermons, orations, discussions, learned volumes, works of art, and songs of praise, than the whole army of great men of ancient and modern times.

"Born in a manger, and crucified as a malefactor, He now

controls the destinies of the civilized world, and rules a spiritual empire which embraces one third of the inhabitants of the globe. There never was in this world a life so unpretending, modest, and lowly in its outward form and condition, and yet producing such extraordinary effects upon all ages, nations, and classes of men. The annals of history furnish no other example of such complete and astounding success, in spite of the absence of these material, social, literary, and artistic powers and influences which are indispensable to success for mere man. Christ stands, in this respect also, solitary and alone among all the heroes of history, and presents to us an unsolvable problem, unless we admit Him to be more than a man, even the eternal Son of God."—"*The Person of Christ,*" *Philip Schaff, page 33.*

CHAPTER THREE

IN THE SHADOW OF THE CROSS

IN FIXING our gaze upon Jesus, our beholding should be especially focused upon the closing scenes of His earthly life. We should consider Him as He passed through the struggle in Gethsemane; stood on trial before Annas, Caiaphas, Herod, and Pilate; and in His crucifixion and death. While we should behold Jesus all through His earthly life and ministry and consider Him from every possible viewpoint, our gaze should become more intense as we near the closing scenes that climaxed the plan of redemption. Just as the interest and enthusiasm of an audience increases as the drama approaches and climaxes in the last tragic scene, so should ours as we behold the Hero of heroes in the most gripping and tragic of all the scenes in the great drama of life and death. It is indeed the world's master tragedy.

It was during these tragic events that the divine nature of Jesus was most clearly manifested, and a supreme example set for our imitation. The apostle Peter declared that "Christ also suffered for us, leaving us an example, that ye should follow His steps: who did no sin, neither was guile found in His mouth: who, when He was reviled, reviled not again; when He suffered, He threatened not; but committed Himself to Him that judgeth righteously: who His own self bare our sins in His own body on the tree, that we, being dead to sins, should live unto righteousness: by whose stripes ye were healed." 1 Peter 2: 21-24.

While we should imitate the example of Jesus from His birth to Calvary, the spirit that we most need is that which took Him through the horror of great darkness to a triumphant death on the cross. This is the admonition of the apostle Paul: "Let the very spirit which was in Christ Jesus be in you also. From the beginning He had the nature of God. Yet He did not regard equality with God as something at which He should grasp. Nay He stripped Himself of His glory, and took on Him the nature of a bondservant by becoming a man like other men. And being recognized as truly human, He humbled Himself and even stooped to die; yes, to die on a cross. It is in consequence of this that God has also so highly exalted Him, and has conferred on Him the Name which is supreme above every other." Philippians 2: 5-9, Weymouth. Oh that we all possessed such a mind and spirit!

God's Remedy for Sin

As soon as there was sin, there was a Saviour, for the plan of salvation was laid before the foundation of the world. Since salvation and the cross are inseparable, the shadow of the cross reaches back to the entrance of sin, for the cross is the antidote for sin. When Jesus offered to pay the redemption price with the sacrifice of His own life, and this offer was accepted by the Father, He entered the shadow of the cross, and His crucifixion sufferings began; to all intents and purposes He was slain. This is what the revelator meant when he declared that Jesus is "the Lamb slain from the foundation of the world." Revelation 13: 8.

It is for this reason that the sufferings of Christ because of sin did not begin or end with His visit to this world. The cross of Calvary is but a revelation to our dull senses of the awful sufferings that sin, from its very inception, has brought to the heart of God. Because of His perfect knowledge of the future, in one sense the Son of God walked in the shadow of the cross from all eternity; but this shadow gradually deepened until it reached the substance on Golgotha. The shadow of the cross reaches both ways, to the beginning and to the end of sin. Since His death, Christ has continued in its shadow. He is still the slain Lamb. More than sixty years after His ascension Jesus was seen by John in vision as "a Lamb as it had been slain." See Revelation 5: 6. Not until sin and sinners are no more will the Son of God fully escape from the shadow of the emblem of ignominy and shame. By our sins we still crucify to ourselves "the Son of God afresh, and put Him to an open shame." Hebrews 6: 6.

Throughout all the eternity of the future, Christ will be praised as the Lamb of God. The apostle John was given a vision of the redeemed state. He heard the unnumbered angelic host, "saying with a loud voice, Worthy is the Lamb that was slain to receive power, and riches, and wisdom, and strength, and honor, and glory, and blessing. And every creature which is in heaven, and on the earth, and under the earth, and such as are in the sea, and all that are in them, heard I saying, Blessing, and honor, and glory, and power, be unto Him that sitteth upon the throne, and unto the Lamb forever and ever." Revelation 5: 12, 13.

The cross of Christ will be the science and the song of the redeemed throughout the endless ages of eternity. In Christ glorified the redeemed will see Christ crucified. He will always carry the marks of His crucifixion. One of the Old Testament prophets, in describing the second advent of Christ, declares that as He comes in the clouds of heaven He will have "horns," or "bright beams," coming out of His side and hands where were the wounds made by the spear and the nails. See Habakkuk 3: 3-6, margin. Another says that when the redeemed reach the kingdom "one shall say unto

Him, What are these wounds in Thine hands? Then He shall answer, Those with which I was wounded in the house of My friends." Zechariah 13:6. In all the eternal ages Jesus will carry the marks of His sacrifice for sin. This will not only be a continual reminder of His love, but it will also give assurance that "affliction shall not rise up the second time." Nahum 1:9.

The Great Center

The cross of Calvary is the meeting place of the two eternities. It is the hub where all truths converge and all mysteries are explained. The death of Christ as an atonement for sin is the greatest fact of history, around which all other truths cluster. Every truth revealed in the Scriptures, if they would be properly understood and appreciated, must be studied in the light that streams from Calvary's cross. This is the mystery of godliness that explains all other mysteries. Is it, therefore, any wonder that our study and meditation and beholding of Jesus should be focused upon the closing scenes of His tragic career?

As far as we know, the childhood, youth, and young manhood of Jesus were normal and unclouded by severe storms. The special attacks of Satan upon Him began with His baptism, when He entered upon His mission as the Messiah, or Anointed One. The voice of the Father claiming Jesus as His well-beloved Son and the descent of the Holy Spirit as the evidence that He was a complete victor over sin, together with the ignominious defeat of Satan in the contest in the wilderness, removed all questions in the mind of the enemy as to the identity of Jesus. "Satan had questioned whether Jesus was the Son of God. In his summary dismissal he had proof that he could not gainsay. Divinity flashed through suffering humanity. Satan had no power to resist the command. Writhing with humiliation and rage, he was forced to withdraw from the presence of the world's Redeemer. Christ's victory was as complete as had been the failure of Adam."—"*The Desire of Ages,*" *page 130.*

Although driven from the battlefield as the result of this forty-day contest, Satan's departure was only temporary. He soon returned to renew his attacks, which grew fiercer and more determined as the struggle for the supremacy of the world continued. The archenemy hounded the footsteps of the Redeemer night and day as He traveled toward the cross, and the shadow deepened as He approached the climax that determined the doom of the human race.

As the crisis approached, Jesus said to His disciples: "The hour is come, that the Son of man should be glorified. Verily, verily, I say unto you, Except a corn of wheat fall into the ground and die, it abideth alone: but if it die, it bringeth forth much fruit. . . . Now is My soul troubled; and what shall I say? Father, save Me from this hour: but for this cause came I unto this hour. Father, glorify Thy name. Then came there a voice from heaven, saying, I have both glorified it, and will glorify it again." John 12: 23-28.

The previous chapter of the Gospel of John describes the resurrection of Lazarus and the bitter enmity this mighty miracle created among the Jewish leaders. So many believed on Jesus that the scribes and Pharisees became alarmed, and a meeting of the Sanhedrin was called to plan the death of Christ. This was the beginning of "the time of trouble" for "the Man of Sorrows." The soul of Jesus shrank from the terrible ordeal before Him, and called forth the prayer just quoted. He was tempted to ask for exemption from the anguish; but an assent to such a request would defeat the very purpose of His mission. He remembered that the plan of salvation required His death, and that He had come into the world especially to go through that trying hour. During World War I a wounded American soldier was told by his physician that he could live but a few hours at the most. After a few minutes of silent reflection he was heard to say resignedly, as if he were answering his own thoughts, "Well, that is what I came over here for." To die the death of the cross was what Jesus had come to this world for; why, then, should He pray to escape it?

Victory Through Christ's Death

Then through the eye of faith Jesus saw the results of His mission, and said: "Now is the judgment of this world: now shall the prince of this world be cast out. And I, if I be lifted up from the earth, will draw all men unto Me. This He said, signifying what death He should die." Verses 31-33. It was this vision that gave Him the determination to carry out His purpose, whatever the cost. He was facing the crisis of the world, the decisive battle in the conflict that would decide the fate of the world and who should be its prince and ruler. He knew that if He would draw all unto Him He must be lifted up on the cross. Like the grain of wheat, He must die in order that there might be a harvest. The "all" included the whole universe that had been affected by the revolt of Lucifer. "Having made peace through the blood of His cross, by Him to reconcile all things unto Himself; by Him, I say, whether they be things in earth, or things in heaven." Colossians 1:20.

Jesus knew that the effects of the curse of sin on all creation could be counteracted in no other way. His death on Calvary alone could destroy the influence of Satan and reconcile the world, the angels, and the universe to God. While only one third of the angelic host had joined in the open revolt, and only one world had fallen under the withering curse of sin, the loyal angels and the inhabitants of the unfallen worlds could not fully understand the meaning of the revolt or the terrible nature of sin. It was the events of the crisis hour that took Jesus through Gethsemane, the judgment halls of Annas, Caiaphas, Herod, and Pilate, and to the cross of Calvary, that erased every question, and thus brought about complete reconciliation. The death of Christ accomplished far more than the salvation of this world. The restoration of perfect love, unity, and loyalty could be accomplished only by way of the cross; and, setting His face like a flint, Jesus went boldly into the darker shadows that ended only with the cry, "It is finished."

CHAPTER FOUR

THE GETHSEMANE STRUGGLE

Being the true paschal Lamb, the One to whom all the types and shadows in the Levitical system pointed forward, it was appropriate that Jesus should be sacrificed at the time of the Passover. Little did the Jews realize that this was the last Passover festival that would ever have any significance. In the crucifixion of the Messiah all types met their antitype and all shadows merged into their substance. While celebrating this last Passover with His disciples, Jesus instituted the new ordinances, or memorials, which would point back to the great center as the others had pointed forward.

The place of this last meeting was in an "upper room," which some believe was in the home of John Mark and his mother Mary, on the outskirts of Jerusalem. See Acts 12:12. The time was soon after sunset, the evening and beginning of the fourteenth of Nisan, thought to correspond to the sixth of April in the year of our Lord 31 A. D. It was a sad farewell gathering, for, during the entire evening, Jesus was visibly troubled. It was evident to all who knew Him that some great crisis was impending. It was at this time that He began to reveal the dark vision that was gripping His soul. "During the evening, a bitter anxiety, an awful melancholy, seized the devoted band, whose number, thirteen, even today inspires superstitious dread."—"*The Trial of Jesus*," *Walter M. Chandler, vol. 1, p. 222.*

Following the departure of Judas to betray his Master, Jesus began His farewell instruction, or sermon, to the eleven. See John 13:31-38; 14; 15; 16. The discourse in the upper room was followed by the singing of a Passover hymn, a selection from Psalms 113 to 118, for these were the usual Passover hymns. "When they had sung an hymn, they went out into the Mount of Olives." Matthew 26: 30. The disciples then followed Jesus out into the darkness of that tragic night, the night that determined the fate of our world and its future sovereignty.

The range of mountains known as Olivet lies east of Jerusalem, the central summit being the Mount of Ascension, which is 2,641 feet above sea level. It must have been between ten and eleven o'clock when Jesus and the eleven disciples left the upper room, and, wending their way through the narrow streets of Jerusalem, passed through one of the east gates. As they walked on, Jesus continued to teach His followers and to speak words of comfort and cheer. Finally, "with strong, hopeful words the Saviour ended His instruction. Then He poured out the burden of His soul in prayer for His disciples"—the memorable prayer of John 17. Between the city and the Mount of Olives was a valley, or gorge, known as the Kedron, and through which flowed, during the rainy season, a brook by the same name. Under the light of a full moon the little group descended into the canyon, crossed the dry bed of the Kedron, and ascended the west slope of Olivet. That this retired spot was one of Christ's sanctuaries for meditation and prayer is evident from John 18: 2 and Luke 21: 37.

"They came to a place which was named Gethsemane: and He saith to His disciples, Sit ye here, while I shall pray." Mark 14: 32. Near the foot of the Mount of Olives was a grove, or orchard, of olive trees, which was called the Garden of Gethsemane. The name means "oil press" because in the orchard was a rock-hewn trough in which the olives were crushed or trodden, causing the rich oil to flow into a lower vat. Whether this was a public garden or park, or belonged to a friend of Jesus, we do not know, but we can be certain that the place was often visited by the Master and His disciples. Leaving eight of His disciples at the entrance of the garden, with the instruction, "Sit ye here, while I go and pray yonder" (Matthew 26:36), Jesus took Peter, James, and John, and led them farther into the grove. These three seemed to be closer to Jesus than the others, and had thus been given special privileges. They had before been selected to witness the resurrection of the daughter of Jairus and the transfiguration of Jesus on the mount, and now they were again chosen from among the others to be with Him during the hours of His terrible agony. These three were among the first to be called to discipleship; they had been closest to Christ during His ministry; and they were the most prominent during apostolic church history. Sadly they followed their Lord into the shadows of the olive trees to the place of spiritual conflict.

Every great war has its decisive battle, the pivot on which turns the tide of the fortunes of war to the victor. The struggle between Christ and Satan over the dominion of this earth and man had been long and bitter. The first great battle in heaven, which resulted in the defeat of Lucifer and his dethronement as the anointed covering cherub, and the forty-day contest in the wilderness at the beginning of Christ's ministry, which again brought victory to the cause of righteousness, were epoch-making events. But the decisive battle in the long war was fought in the Garden of Gethsemane. It was "the battle of the giants," fought in desperation because of its eternal consequences. It tested the faith, courage, and love of Christ to the utmost; but from it

He emerged triumphant, though with garments stained with blood and hands and feet scarred with wounds.

It was Christ's longing for human sympathy and companionship during His agony that caused Him to ask the three who were nearest and dearest to Him to accompany Him to the place of prayer, which was also the place of battle. As the four passed into the stillness and solitude of the garden, the moonlight filtered through the network of new spring olive leaves, which, with their branches, were emblems of peace. Presently Jesus stopped and told the three that they could follow Him no farther. He said to them: "My soul is exceeding sorrowful, even unto death: tarry ye here, and watch with Me." Matthew 26: 38. He then went on "about a stone's cast"—alone. While passing through deep waters we desire our friends to be near, and our closest friends to be very near; but even they cannot fully share our sorrows. The final struggle in the spiritual warfare must be endured alone. The poet has expressed this fact in a beautiful way:

"Our crosses are hewn from different trees,
But we all must have our Calvaries;
We may climb the height from a different side,
But we each go up to be crucified.
As we scale the steep, another may share
The dreadful load that our shoulders bear;
But the costliest sorrow is all our own,
For on the summit we bleed alone."

The various Gospel writers seem to tax their descriptive powers to the utmost in attempting to picture the indescribable anguish of their Master in the Gethsemane struggle. "He took with Him Peter and the two sons of Zebedee, and began to be sorrowful and very heavy. Then saith He unto them, My soul is exceeding sorrowful, even unto death: tarry ye here, and watch with Me. And He went a little farther, and fell on His face, and prayed, saying, O My Father, if it be possible, let this cup pass from Me: nevertheless not as I will, but as Thou wilt." Matthew 26: 37-39. "And He was withdrawn from them about a stone's cast, and kneeled down, and prayed, saying, Father, if Thou be willing, remove this cup from Me: nevertheless not My will, but Thine, be done. And there appeared an angel unto Him from heaven, strengthening Him. And being in an agony He prayed more earnestly: and His sweat was as it were great drops of blood falling down to the ground." Luke 22: 41-44. The use of the "cup" as the symbol of suffering and death had its origin with the ancient custom of giving condemned criminals a cup of poison and compelling them to drink it. Satan has given to every human being the deadly poison of sin; and, in order that we might escape the fatal effects of this cup of death, Jesus took the cup apportioned to guilty man, and drank it to its bitter dregs; thus He tasted "death for every man." He died in our stead.

Sin Bearer for a Lost World

It seems from the description that Jesus first kneeled and then fell on His face as if He were being crushed under some invisible weight. The pent-up sorrow that had been gathering for some time seemed suddenly to burst forth. The disciples described Jesus during this struggle as being "sore amazed," "very heavy," and "exceeding sorrowful." In His terrible isolation it seemed to Jesus that even heaven was forsaking Him, and that its lights were going out and leaving Him to go through the valley of the shadow of death alone in a horror of great darkness. He was bearing the sins of the whole world, and their awful weight was crushing out His life. The Lord had "laid on Him the iniquity of us all." Jesus was taking the place of lost sinners in order to destroy the author of sin, and thus deliver them from fearful bondage. See Hebrews 2: 14, 15.

Through the psalmist the Messiah thus foretold His own suffering: "The sorrows of death compassed Me, and the floods of ungodly men made Me afraid. The sorrows of hell compassed Me about: the snares of death prevented Me. In My distress I called upon the Lord, and cried unto My God: He heard My voice out of His temple, and My cry came before Him, even into His ears." Psalm 18: 4-6. More than thirty years after His passion one of the apostles thus described the Gethsemane experience: "Jesus during His earthly life offered up prayers and entreaties, crying aloud and weeping as He pleaded with Him who was able to bring Him in safety out of death, and He was delivered from the terror from which He shrank. Although He was God's Son, yet He learned obedience from the sufferings which He endured; and so, having been made perfect, He became to all who obey Him the source and giver of eternal salvation. For God Himself addresses Him as a High Priest forever, belonging to the order of Melchizedek." Hebrews 5: 7-10, Weymouth.

It was not from the thought of physical death that Jesus shrank in terror, and from which He wept and prayed to be delivered. It was from the sinner's death as the wages of sin—the second and eternal death; the death that brings an eternal separation from God and heaven. In taking the place of lost sinners, Jesus had to enter that "outer darkness" where there is "weeping and gnashing of teeth." See

Matthew 8:11, 12; 13:42, 50; 24:50, 51; 25:30. Jesus passed through all the terrors of those who realize that they are eternally lost, without one ray of hope. He fully met the penalty of the broken law, with all the mental and soul anguish that the experience involves.

One writer gives the following graphic description of the Gethsemane struggle of the Son of God: "Now had come the hour of the power of darkness. Now His voice was heard on the still evening air, not in tones of triumph, but full of human anguish. . . . The humanity of the Son of God trembled in that trying hour. He prayed not now for His disciples that their faith might not fail, but for His own tempted, agonized soul. The awful moment had come—that moment which was to decide the destiny of the world. The fate of humanity trembled in the balance. Christ might even now refuse to drink the cup apportioned to guilty man. It was not yet too late. He might wipe the bloody sweat from His brow, and leave man to perish in his iniquity. He might say, Let the transgressor receive the penalty of his sin, and I will go back to My Father. Will the Son of God drink the bitter cup of humiliation and agony? Will the innocent suffer the consequences of the curse of sin, to save the guilty? The words fall tremblingly from the pale lips of Jesus, 'O My Father, if this cup may not pass away from Me, except I drink it, Thy will be done.' "—*"The Desire of Ages," page 690.*

CHAPTER FIVE

THE DIVINE AGONY

ONE OF the Gospel writers gives the following description of the threefold prayer struggle of Jesus in the Garden of Gethsemane: "He said, Abba, Father, all things are possible unto Thee; take away this cup from Me: nevertheless not what I will, but what Thou wilt. And He cometh, and findeth them sleeping, and saith unto Peter, Simon, sleepest thou? couldest not thou watch one hour? Watch ye and pray, lest ye enter into temptation. The spirit truly is ready, but the flesh is weak. And again He went away, and prayed, and spake the same words. And when He returned, He found them asleep again, (for their eyes were heavy,) neither wist they what to answer Him. And He cometh the third time, and saith unto them, Sleep on now, and take your rest: it is enough, the hour is come; behold, the Son of man is betrayed into the hands of sinners." Mark 14:36-41.

It is estimated that these three seasons of prayer consumed about two hours. As the divine Presence was being withdrawn, Jesus in His desperation sought the sympathy and companionship of the three disciples who had been asked to watch and pray with Him. Three times He went to them hoping to find them interested enough in His agony of soul to be awake and praying; but, instead, He found them sleeping as peacefully as if there were no crisis in which their own eternal destinies were involved. Addressing Peter, Jesus said: "Simon, sleepest thou? couldest not thou watch one hour?" This deserved rebuke was doubtless given to Peter because of his previous boasting. When Jesus foretold His death and that all of them would forsake Him in the hour of His greatest need, Peter had boastfully said, "Though all men shall be offended because of Thee, yet will I never be offended." "Though I should die with Thee, yet will I not deny Thee." "And he [Peter] said unto Him, Lord, I am ready to go with Thee, both into prison, and to death." Matthew 26: 33, 35; Luke 22: 33.

The mental agony of Jesus was so great that "His sweat was as it were great drops of blood falling down to the ground." Luke 22: 14. Critics declare that "as it were" proves that it was not really blood. The "as it were," however, applied to the sweat rather than to the blood. The blood oozed out of the pores of His skin, and fell to the ground "as it were sweat," or in the likeness of sweat. Those who declare that the writer drew upon his imagination in describing the agony of Jesus forget that Luke was a physician, and as such was especially impressed with this strange physical disturbance. Another might easily have been mistaken regarding this experience, but not a physician. This is doubtless the reason why Luke is the only one of the four Gospel writers who mentions this occurrence. Another New Testament writer doubtless had the bloody sweat in mind when he declared that Jesus "resisted unto blood, striving against sin." Hebrews 12: 4. The Gethsemane struggle must also be included in the description found in Isaiah 63: 1-3: "Who is this that cometh from Edom, with dyed garments from Bozrah? this that is glorious in His apparel, traveling in the greatness of His strength? I that speak in righteousness, mighty to save. Wherefore art Thou red in Thine apparel, and Thy garments like him that treadeth in the wine fat? I have trodden the wine press alone; and of the people there was none with Me." It was the bloody sweat more than anything else that dyed or stained with blood the garments of the Messiah.

While the sweating of blood is a very rare occurrence, it is not unknown to history and to medical science. It is known to medical authorities as diapedesis. The word is defined by Webster thus: "The passage of the corpuscular elements of the blood from the blood vessels into the surrounding tissues." A few notable cases have been left on record by historians and physicians where persons under great physical strain, mental anguish, or intense fear, have actually "sweat blood." Since this is true, it was certainly the most natural thing that could have happened to Jesus while passing through a season of physical suffering and mental fear and anguish so terrible that it surpasses the utmost stretch of the human mind to portray.

The Cause of Diapedesis

Of the possibility and cause of diapedesis, G. H. Kannegiesser, a German physician, wrote: " 'Violent mental excitement, . . . and in like manner sudden terror, or intense fear, forces out a sweat. . . . If the mind is seized with a sudden fear of death, the sweat, owing to the excessive degree of constriction, often becomes bloody.' "—*German "Ephemerides," quoted by William Stroud, M. D., in "The Physical Cause of the Death of Christ," page 86.* Dr. Stroud was at one time the President of the Royal Medical Society of Scotland, and his book was endorsed by some of the leading physicians of the British Isles. His book was first published in 1847.

Of this rare occurrence another physician wrote: "Of all the maladies which affect cutaneous transpiration, diapedesis, or sweating of blood, is the most singular; so much so indeed, that its existence has been doubted, although several well-authenticated cases are on record, both in the ancient and modern annals of medicine. It is mentioned by Theophrastus, Aristotle, and Lucan. . . . The base Charles IX of France sank under this disorder, as stated by Mezeray. The same historian relates the case of a governor of a town taken by storm, who was condemned to die, but was seized with a profuse sweating of blood the moment he beheld the scaffold. Lombard mentions a general who was affected in a similar manner on losing a battle. . . . It is probable that the strange disorder arises from a violent commotion of the nervous system, turning the streams of blood out of their natural course, and forcing the red particles into the cutaneous excretories."—"*Curiosities of Medical Experience,*" *J. G. Millingen, M. D., vol. 2, pp. 338-342. (Stroud.)*

S. A. D. Tissot, a Swiss physician and author who lived between 1728 and 1779, reported the case of "a sailor who was so alarmed by a storm, that through fear he fell down, and his face sweated blood; which during the whole continuance of the storm returned like ordinary sweat, as fast as it was wiped away."—"*Traite des Nerfs,*" *pages 279, 280. (Stroud.)* Dr. Schenck, a German physician, cites the case of "a nun who fell into the hands of soldiers; and, on seeing herself encompassed with swords and daggers threatening instant death, was so terrified and agitated, that she discharged blood from every part of her body, and died of hemorrhage in the sight of her assailants."—*Joannes Schenck a Grafenberg, in* "*Observ. Medic.,*" *lib. 3, p. 458. (Stroud.)*

Writing of the death of Charles IX of France, F. M. Voltaire said: "The disease which carried him off is very uncommon; his blood flowed from all his pores. This malady, of which there are some examples, is the result either of excessive fear, furious passion, or of a violent and melancholic temperament."—"*Œuvres Completes,*" *vol. 18, pp. 531, 532. (Stroud.)*

De Mezeray, a French historian, declared of the same case: "During the last two weeks of his life, his constitution made strange efforts. He was affected with spasms and convulsions of extreme violence. He tossed and agitated himself continually, and his blood gushed from all the outlets of his body, even from the pores of his skin, so that on one occasion he was found bathed in a bloody sweat."—"*Histoire de France,*" *vol. 3, p. 306. (Stroud.)*

The French historian, De Thou, tells of "'an Italian officer who commanded at Monte-Maro, a fortress of Piedmont, during the warfare in 1552, between Henry II of France and the emperor Charles V. This officer, having been treacherously seized by order of the hostile general, and threatened with public execution unless he surrendered the place, was so agitated at the prospect of an ignominious death, that he sweated blood from every part of his body.'" The same author also wrote of a young Florentine at Rome, unjustly put to death by order of Pope Sixtus V, and concludes the narrative as follows: "'When the youth was led forth to execution, he excited the commiseration of many, and through excess of grief, was observed to shed bloody tears, and to discharge blood instead of sweat from his whole body.'"—"*The Physical Cause of the Death of Christ,*" *Stroud, pages 86, 87.* Other historic and scientific testimony might be given, but this is sufficient to prove that the sweating of blood is not only possible under excessive pain and fear, but that it has actually happened on many different occasions. Thus, once more, destructive Biblical criticism has been silenced by the facts of history and science.

Each prayer of the Son of God in the garden ended with an expression of complete submission to His Father's will. This unwavering faith and unquestioning submission won Him the victory in the Gethsemane struggle. His triumph brought calmness to His soul, and the peace of victory settled down over the battlefield. Gabriel came to give Him strength to go through to the cross.

It was "the joy that was set before Him" that made it possible for Jesus to endure the cross, and despise the shame, so that He could sit "down at the right hand of the throne of God." Hebrews 12:2. It was in the garden that Jesus saw "of the travail of His soul," and was "satisfied" to pay the redemption price. Isaiah 53:11. It was then that He caught a glimpse of the future, and of the happiness of those who would be saved through His humiliation and death. By faith His ear caught the triumphant shout of the redeemed, and He heard the ransomed singing the song of Moses and the Lamb. In this crisis hour, when the fate of a lost world hung in the balance, Jesus doubtless thought of what His failure would mean to Enoch, Elijah, and Moses, who were already in heaven because of their faith that He would keep His covenant with them. Every slain lamb from the very gates of the lost Paradise had been a promise that the true and antitypical Lamb would also die.

These were some of the contemplations that brought Jesus to the final and irrevocable decision to continue the struggle and, at whatever cost, go on to Calvary. Speaking of this great decision, a noted Italian advocate, deputator to the Italian parliament and advocate of the court of Tuscany wrote: "And while the olive branches, symbols of peace, sole condition of love and mildness among men, rustled and swayed in the night wind under the immensity of the starry heavens, Jesus tasted the bitter cup overflowing with the tears and blood of unredeemed humanity, and resolved to drink it to the dregs."—"*The Trial of Jesus*," *Giovanni Rosadi, page 113.*

In describing the midnight struggle of Jesus and the agony that tortured His mind and soul, Dr. David Russell of Dundee, Scotland, wrote: "His heart was preternaturally fired within Him, so as to force a passage through the body for His rarefied blood; for His sweat was as it were great drops of blood falling down to the ground. The agony of His soul must have been bitter beyond conception, when such was its effect upon His body in the open air, at midnight, and when they who were within found it necessary to defend themselves against the cold. His firm heart was ready to break, and immediate death was threatened; but knowing that much remained to be accomplished, it was His prayer that the cup might for a time pass from Him. His prayer was heard. An angel appeared to strengthen Him, and He regained composure to act with propriety before His judges and the people, and to suffer what He endured before He reached the cross. On the cross the scene of Gethsemane was renewed;—the cup was again presented to Him, and there He drank it to the very dregs."—"*Letters, Chiefly Practical and Consolatory*," *vol. 1, pp. 7-9.* (*Stroud.*)

It is evident that Jesus was dying when He said, "My soul is exceeding sorrowful, even unto death." He was entering the death throes, and would have died of a broken or ruptured heart when, in answer to His prayer, the cup of death was temporarily removed and Gabriel was sent to give Him strength to endure the bloody and tragic ordeal that ended on the cross, where was paid the last and greatest installment of the price of man's redemption from sin.

CHAPTER SIX

THE MIDNIGHT ARREST

AFTER the third season of prayer in the Garden of Gethsemane Jesus returned to the three sleeping disciples and said: "The hour is at hand, and the Son of man is betrayed into the hands of sinners. Rise, let us be going: behold, he is at hand that doth betray Me." Matthew 26: 45, 46. No sooner had Jesus spoken than the darkness began to be dispersed by the lights from the lanterns and torches, and the stillness of the garden retreat was broken by the noise of the approaching mob under the leadership of Judas the betrayer. The eight disciples who were left at the entrance of the garden doubtless fled at the approach of the rabble.

"And Judas also, which betrayed Him, knew the place: for Jesus ofttimes resorted thither with His disciples. Judas then, having received a band of men and officers from the chief priests and Pharisees, cometh thither with lanterns and torches and weapons." "And while He yet spake, lo, Judas, one of the twelve, came, and with him a great multitude with swords and staves, from the chief priests and elders of the people. Now he that betrayed Him gave them a sign, saying, Whomsoever I shall kiss, that same is He: hold Him fast. And forthwith he came to Jesus, and said, Hail, Master; and kissed Him. And Jesus said unto him, Friend, wherefore art thou come? Then came they, and laid hands on Jesus, and took Him." John 18: 2, 3; Matthew 26: 47-50.

The arrest of Jesus took place soon after midnight of Nisan 14, according to the Hebrew calendar, or on April 7, according to Roman time. The Hebrews began their day at sunset and the Romans at midnight. It is evident that "the band of men and officers" who arrested Jesus was a part of the temple guard, a large body of whom was required to police the temple buildings and grounds, especially during the time of national festivals when multitudes of worshipers came to Jerusalem from all parts of the then-known world. Luke speaks of them as "captains of the temple." Luke 22:52. Both Matthew and Mark declare that the officers and men came with Judas from the chief priests and scribes and elders of the people. John says that Judas "received a band of men and officers from the chief priests and Pharisees," and that "the band and the captain and officers of the Jews took Jesus, and bound Him." John 18:3, 12.

It seems evident, however, that the temple guard was accompanied and assisted by a small detachment of Roman soldiers so as to make the arrest legal and to avoid a misunderstanding with the Roman authorities. The temple guard had jurisdiction only within the precincts of the temple. The Jewish leaders would hardly have run the risk of sending out a mob at that time of night without arrangements with Pilate or the centurion in charge of the Roman garrison. The Roman officials would never have permitted "a great multitude" to leave the city on such a mission without sending along with them a company of soldiers to preserve order and to observe the conduct of the mob. The danger of insurrection at the time of the Passover was especially serious, and to guard against it extra soldiers were brought to the city for patrol duty. Pilate himself came from Cæsarea to guard the interests of Rome. Every gathering of the Jews that resembled a mob or gave suspicion of an insurrection was immediately dispersed, often with great violence. The Jews at this time were restless with the spirit of revolt, and their every move was watched by the Romans.

A number of authors make mention of Roman soldiers as assisting the temple guard in making the arrest. Walter M. Chandler, a well-known New York attorney, writes: "Jesus was arrested about midnight in Gethsemane by a band of temple officers and Roman soldiers guided by Judas." "This midnight mob, led by Judas, was made up of Roman soldiers, the temple guard, and stragglers from along the way."—*"The Trial of Jesus," vol. 1, pp. xvi, 225.* Ernest Renan declared that "it was the guards of the temple, armed with staves, a kind of police under the control of the priests. They were supported by a detachment of Roman soldiers with their swords."—*"The Life of Jesus," page 344.* Geikie thus describes the midnight event: "The authorities remained in permanent session till the arrest was effected, and at once detached part of the temple watch, a body acting as the police of the temple and only armed, in a few cases, with wooden batons or clubs. . . . The high priest had, therefore, communicated with Pilate, representing, doubtless, that he proposed the arrest of a false messiah, dangerous to the Roman power, and feared a rescue. A 'band' had, therefore, been told off from the troops in Antonia."—*"The Life and Words of Christ," page 742.*

"Jesus therefore, knowing all things that should come upon Him, went forth, and said unto them, Whom seek ye? They answered Him, Jesus of Nazareth. Jesus saith unto them, I am He. And Judas also, which betrayed Him, stood with them. As soon then as He had said unto them, I am He, they went backward, and fell to the ground." John 18: 4-6. Just before His arrest Jesus not only demonstrated to the mob that He could easily escape if He so desired, but He also gave them a final proof of His divinity. A ray of His divine glory was permitted to flash through His humanity, and the murderous throng staggered backward and fell as dead men to the ground. As His enemies lay prostrate and helpless at His feet, the temporarily glorified Messiah stood calm and self-possessed in their midst, with no effort to escape their clutches. It was a final appeal to Judas and to those who claimed to be the elect of God.

The Courage of Peter

As the prostrate rabble began to arise and rally their forces to complete their mission, Peter felt that his opportunity had come. He was anxious to atone for having gone to sleep while Jesus was praying, and also to make good his boast that he would stand by Jesus and even lay down his life for His sake. "Then Simon Peter having a sword drew it, and smote the high priest's servant, and cut off his right ear. The servant's name was Malchus." John 18: 10. No one can question Peter's courage. Singlehanded he attacked the whole mob, including armed soldiers. He could not watch and pray for even one hour, but he could fight a whole multitude. All alone he courageously faced an angry and determined mob, and then later during the same night retreated ignominiously before the pointing finger of a maid. He was a physical hero and at the same time a spiritual weakling and a moral coward. To this day the braggart who begins with boasting and overconfidence and ends in failure and defeat is said to have "petered out." There are many in the modern church with the characteristics of Peter. But there is hope for them as there was for Peter. Peter's weakest point finally became his strongest.

"Then said Jesus unto him, Put up again thy sword into his place: for all they that take the sword shall perish with the sword. Thinkest thou that I cannot now pray to My Father, and He shall presently give Me more than twelve legions of angels?" Matthew 26: 52, 53. This rebuke, together with Christ's miracle of healing the wounded ear, prevented Peter from getting into very serious trouble. This miracle was the second evidence of Christ's divinity given in connection with His arrest. The statement of Jesus regarding the use of the sword was also a rebuke to the armed guards and soldiers. They would some day perish by the same weapons they were now using against Him. Little did they dream how soon this terrible prediction would be fulfilled to the Jews by the Romans, and later to the Romans by the barbarians of the north. The principle that men perish by the very weapons they employ against others is the unfailing law of men and nations. "He that leadeth into captivity shall go into captivity: he that killeth with the sword must be killed with the sword." Revelation 13: 10.

Jesus reminded Peter and the mob that He had plenty of help available. On request, He would be given "more than twelve legions of angels," or a legion each for Himself and His eleven disciples, in contrast with the little band of soldiers who took part in the arrest. A Roman legion averaged 6,000 soldiers, and some legions contained as many as 9,000. Between 75,000 and 100,000 mighty angels "that excel in strength" would, at the request of Christ, have been sent from the army of heaven to deliver Him from His foes. Only one of these celestial beings had been sufficient to cause the whole multitude to fall prostrate and helpless to the ground a few moments before. They were unable to complete their plans until the protection was withdrawn. Unless Jesus chose to submit, no earthly power was able to molest Him.

In answer to the question of Jesus, "Whom seek ye?" the rabble answered, "Jesus of Nazareth." Jesus then said, "I have told you that I am He: if therefore ye seek Me, let these go their way." "And they all forsook Him, and fled. And there followed Him a certain young man, having a linen cloth cast about his naked body; and the young men laid hold on him: and he left the linen cloth, and fled from them naked." John 18: 8; Mark 14: 50-52. It is believed that the young man mentioned was John Mark, who had come with Jesus and the disciples from the upper room. Mark is the only one who records this incident, and he designates the person as "a certain young man." This was a big event in his young life, but in the estimation of the other writers was too unimportant to record. Perhaps they did not witness it, as they, too, were fleeing for their lives.

It seems that John was the bravest of them all, for, after his first flight, he returned and remained as close as possible to his Master through the remainder of the night and until His death and burial on the afternoon of the next day. No wonder he is designated as "the disciple whom Jesus loved." Just before He died on the cross, Jesus committed His mother to the care of John. Friends who remain loyal through a crisis are very few, but, because of their devotion, they are dearly beloved.

The Arrest Illegal

According to Hebrew law the arrest of Jesus was illegal on four separate counts. In the first place, all legal proceedings, including arrests, were forbidden by night. "It was a well-established and inflexible rule of Hebrew law that proceedings in capital trials could not be had at night. This provision did not apply simply to the proceedings of the trial after the prisoner had been arraigned and the examination had been begun. We have it upon the authority of Dupin ["Jesus Devant Caiphe et Pilate"] that it applied to the entire proceedings, from the arrest to the execution. The great French advocate explicitly states that the arrest was illegal because it was made at night."—"*The Trial of Jesus,*" *Chandler, vol. 1, pp. 226, 227.*

In the second place, the use of a traitor, and thus an accomplice, in effecting an arrest or securing a conviction was forbidden by Hebrew law. There was no such thing as "turning state's evidence" in Hebrew jurisprudence. This rule was based on Leviticus 19: 16-18. "The testimony of an accomplice is not permissible by rabbinic law, . . . and no man's *life*, nor his *liberty*, nor his *reputation* can be endangered by the malice of one who has confessed himself a criminal."—"*The Criminal Jurisprudence of the Ancient Hebrews,*" *S. Mendelsohn, page 274.* (*Chandler.*) Of this rule of Hebrew law Chandler says: "In modern jurisdictions, accomplice testimony has been and is allowed. The judicial authorities, however, have always regarded it with distrust, and we might say with deep-seated suspicion. . . . In the American States the testimony of an accomplice is admissible, but must be corroborated in order to sustain a conviction. This is the general rule. . . . The ancient Hebrews forbade the use of accomplice testimony. . . . The arrest of Jesus was ordered upon the supposition that He was a criminal; this same supposition would have made Judas, who had aided, encouraged, and abetted Jesus in the propagation of His faith, an accomplice. If Judas was not an accomplice, Jesus was innocent, and His arrest was an outrage, and therefore illegal."—"*The Trial of Jesus,*" *vol. 1, pp. 228, 229.*

In the third place, the arrest was not legal, because it

was not the result of a legal mandate. Chandler declares that "His capture was not the result of a legal mandate from a court whose intentions were to conduct a legal trial for the purpose of reaching a righteous judgment."—*Id., page* 237. "This arrest, effected in the night between Thursday and Friday. the last day of the life of Jesus, on Nisan 14, according to the Hebrew calendar, was the execution of an illegal and factious resolution of the Sanhedrin. . . . There was no idea of apprehending a citizen in order to try him upon a charge which after sincere and regular judgment might be found just or unfounded; the intention was simply to seize a man and do away with him. The arrest was not a preventive measure such as might lawfully precede trial and condemnation: it was an executive act, accomplished in view of a sentence to be pronounced without legal justification."—"*The Trial of Jesus,*" *Rosadi, page 114.*

In the fourth place, according to the rules of Hebrew law, it was illegal to bind an uncondemned man. The record says that "the band and the captain and officers of the Jews took Jesus, and bound Him. and led Him away to Annas." John 18: 12, 13. Thus, in connection with the midnight arrest of Jesus in the Garden of Gethsemane, took place the first four of a series of more than a score of illegal acts that made the entire proceeding the greatest travesty on justice in all the annals of mankind.

CHAPTER SEVEN

THE PRELIMINARY HEARINGS

AFTER being securely bound by the temple guard in the Garden of Gethsemane, Jesus was first taken to the palace of Annas. Annas had been appointed high priest by the Roman legate Quirinus in the year 6 A. D. Seven years later he was deposed from his high office by the procurator Valerius Gratus for imposing and executing capital sentences which had been forbidden by the imperial government. Although he was now only an ex-high priest, he was still the most powerful man in the affairs of the Jews. He still presided over the Sanhedrin at times, and practically dictated its decisions. Five of his sons were successively elevated to the high priesthood, one of them twice. The office of chief pontiff remained in the family of Annas for fifty years; from this the family became known as "the sacerdotal family." Annas was considered by his countrymen to be the most fortunate of men. His five sons were Eleazar, Jonathan, Theophilus, Matthias, and Anan. The only break in the direct reign of the family of Annas was the appointment of his son-in-law, Caiaphas. Josephus declared that Annas was "haughty, audacious, and cruel." At the time Jesus was brought before him, Annas may have been president of the Sanhedrin; that position was not always held by the high priest.

Jesus was subjected to two preliminary hearings before being tried before the supreme tribunal of the Hebrews. The first was before Annas, and took place shortly after midnight. This was followed by another before Caiaphas and perhaps a few members of the Sanhedrin who were the most bitter enemies of Jesus. In these hearings Jesus was closely questioned regarding His disciples and His teachings. "The high priest then asked Jesus of His disciples, and of His doctrine. Jesus answered him, I spake openly to the world; I ever taught in the synagogue, and in the temple, whither the Jews always resort; and in secret have I said nothing. Why askest thou Me? ask them which heard Me, what I have said unto them: behold, they know what I said. And when He had thus spoken, one of the officers which stood by struck Jesus with the palm of his hand, saying, Answerest thou the high priest so? Jesus answered him, If I have spoken evil, bear witness of the evil: but if well, why smitest thou Me? Now Annas had sent Him bound unto Caiaphas the high priest." John 18: 19-24.

Before Annas and Caiaphas

It is not certain whether these verses apply to the preliminary hearing before Annas or Caiaphas, but probably to the former. In this hearing it was hoped that Jesus would make some statement on which an indictment could be based, charging Him with blasphemy or sedition, or both.

This was the first of a series of six trials constituting the world's master judicial burlesque or travesty on justice. Jesus was condemned by two separate tribunals, one Hebrew and the other Roman. Each trial was divided into three parts, the first trial being Christ's hearings before Annas, Caiaphas, and the Sanhedrin. The second trial was before Pilate, Herod, and Pilate again. In the preliminary hearings before Annas and Caiaphas it was hoped that Jesus would incriminate Himself, and furnish evidence which would convict Him before the Jewish tribunal.

"And they that had laid hold on Jesus led Him away to

Caiaphas the high priest, where the scribes and the elders were assembled." Matthew 26: 57. Only John mentions the fact that Jesus was taken before Annas first, and later before Caiaphas. With the high priest were a number of the enemies of Jesus, who had been waiting through the hours of the night for Jesus to be apprehended and brought to trial. It is estimated that Jesus was brought before Caiaphas for a further preliminary hearing about two o'clock in the morning. Joseph Caiaphas had been appointed to the office of high priest by Valerius Gratus in the year 18 A. D. He remained high priest for eleven years, the longest of any of the family of Annas. Caiaphas means "the oppressor," a very appropriate name for the chief enemy of Christ and His apostles. Rosadi declares that "his intellectual caliber was below mediocrity," and that the power he wielded was only nominal. It is evident that Annas was the real power behind the throne as long as he lived. Caiaphas was deposed by Vitellius after the fall of Pilate in 36 A. D. Geikie gives the length of the high priesthood of Caiaphas as seventeen years.

The preliminary hearings before Annas and Caiaphas were illegal on four separate counts. In the first place, they were an infraction of the rule of law that forbade all proceedings by night. M. Dupin, the great French advocate, in speaking of these hearings said: "Now the Jewish law prohibited *all proceedings by night;* there, therefore, was another infraction of the law."—"*The Trial of Jesus Before Caiaphas and Pilate,*" *section 4.* (*Chandler.*)

In the second place, Hebrew law prohibited a judge or a magistrate, sitting alone, from questioning an accused person judicially, or to sit in judgment on his legal rights, either by day or by night. The Hebrews permitted no one-judge courts, their smallest tribunal having three and their largest seventy-one judges. "Be not a sole judge, for there is no sole judge but One," is a well-known statement in the Mishna. It was believed that God alone was capable of judging without counsel.

In the third place, private preliminary hearings were specifically forbidden by Hebrew law. "A principle perpetually reproduced in the Hebrew Scriptures relates to the two conditions of publicity and liberty. An accused man was never subjected to private or secret examination, lest, in his perplexity, he furnish damaging testimony against himself."—"*Histoire des Institutions de Moise,*" *Joseph Salvador, pages 365, 366.* (*Chandler.*) It was to obtain such evidence that Jesus was questioned in these two preliminary hearings. Such hearings were permitted by the Romans to determine whether the accused should go to trial. The same is true in many countries under modern law. The grand jury conducts a preliminary hearing to decide if the accused should be tried before the court. But no such rule was known in Hebrew jurisprudence.

In the fourth place, the striking of Jesus by the officer during the hearing before Annas was "an act of brutality which Hebrew jurisprudence did not tolerate. . . . It was an outrage upon the Hebrew sense of justice and humanity which in its normal state was very pure and lofty."—"*The Trial of Jesus,*" *Chandler, vol. 1, p. 245.* The same writer declared that in His reply to the smiter "Jesus planted Himself squarely upon His legal rights as a Jewish citizen. 'It was in every word the voice of pure Hebrew justice, founded upon the broad principle of their judicial procedure and recalling an unjust judge to the first duty of his great office.' "—*Id., page 246.* Such an act would be illegal in any court in the world. Christ was acting within His legal rights when He refused to answer the questions of the high priest. His statement was an appeal for the legal testimony of witnesses.

Annas and Caiaphas lived virtually under the same roof in the palace of the high priest with only a courtyard between their residences. It was in this court that the rabble awaited the outcome of the hearings before Annas, Caiaphas, and the Sanhedrin. A maid, one of the servants of the palace, kept the door of the court. Among the Hebrews, women were employed as doorkeepers. See Acts 12: 13, and Josephus, "Antiquities," book 7, chap. 2, par. 1. The maid of the palace court was instructed to admit only those who belonged to the mob and those who were known to the household. We are told that John was admitted because he "was known unto the high priest." John 18: 15. Through the intercessions of John, Peter was also admitted into the court.

The Denial of Peter

The night was cold and fires were lighted in the court, and around them the people gathered in groups to warm themselves. Peter was not only cold, but he doubtless was also trembling with fear. He mingled with the group around one of the fires, and tried to act so unconcerned as to give the impression that he was one of them. It seems that he even joined in their conversation in an effort to hide his identity. John made no effort to conceal his relation to Jesus and his concern for His safety, and he experienced no embarrassment.

The maid who admitted him recognized Peter's effort to act a lie, and, pointing her finger at him and in the hearing of all present, she accused him of being one of the disciples of Jesus. Peter's previous attempt to deceive now drove him into a lying denial of his Master. In his chagrin and embarrassment he hurried away to another part of the court, where he was identified by another maid, which led to his second denial. He then moved to another group in his effort to avoid detection and was again recognized, this time by a relative of the high priest's servant whose ear he had cut off during the arrest of Jesus in the garden. To make this denial emphatic and final, Peter declared with an oath that he had never known Jesus. While he was making this shameful denial of his Lord, the crowing of the cock brought him to his senses, and he remembered his boastings and the prophecy of Jesus concerning him.

It is believed that at this very time Jesus was being led through the court from Annas to Caiaphas, and that He heard Peter's vehement denial of ever having known Him. "While the degrading oaths were fresh upon Peter's lips, and the shrill crowing of the cock was still ringing in his ears, the Saviour turned from the frowning judges, and looked full upon His poor disciple. At the same time Peter's eyes were drawn to his Master. In that gentle countenance he read deep pity and sorrow, but there was no anger there. The sight of that pale, suffering face, those quivering lips, that look of compassion and forgiveness, pierced his heart like an arrow. . . . Unable longer to endure the scene, he rushed, heartbroken, from the hall."—"*The Desire of Ages*," *pages* 712, 713.

Peter hurried back to the Garden of Gethsemane, where he had so signally failed his Lord, and, finding the very spot where Jesus had poured out His soul in bitter agony in His contest with the powers of darkness, he fell on his face and "wept bitterly." He could now enter more fully into the experience of Jesus, and he longed for the human sympathy he had failed to give his Master. He, too, must pass through the struggle alone. Jesus had said to him, "When thou art converted, strengthen thy brethren." Luke 22: 32. Peter's Gethsemane experience resulted in his complete conversion, and out of the garden there came a new Peter. All boasting had disappeared, and in its place was a faith and a courage that never failed him. On the day of Pentecost it was a sermon by Peter that brought three thousand souls to the foot of the cross. Fearlessly he charged the Jews with the responsibility of murdering the Son of God.

Every Christian today must meet a similar test. In these days when genuine Christianity is being held in contempt and God's law is despised and trampled underfoot, we shall need a warmth of zeal and a firmness of courage that will hold us steadfast. "To stand in defense of truth and righteousness when the majority forsake us, to fight the battles of the Lord when champions are few—this will be our test. At this time we must gather warmth from the coldness of others, courage from their cowardice, and loyalty from their treason."

CHAPTER EIGHT

THE MEN WHO TRIED JESUS

BEFORE considering the Hebrew trial of Jesus, it will be necessary to get a picture of the tribunal that tried Him and condemned Him to die. Hebrew law was administered in three different courts. The highest, or supreme, tribunal was known as the Great Sanhedrin. It was also called the Council of the Ancients, the Grand Council, and the Senate. It was composed of seventy-one members, and their regular meeting place was in the hall of hewn stone, one of the buildings of the temple group. This great council was both the national parliament and the supreme court of the Jews. In that one body were combined the three departments of government—legislative, judicial, and executive. They made the laws, explained them, and administered them. All the functions of education, government, and religion were exercised by this august body.

The second order of courts was that of the Minor Sanhedrins, each of which had twenty-three judges. Each town of one hundred twenty or more adult male inhabitants was entitled to a Minor Sanhedrin. There were at least two in Jerusalem, which were next to the Great Sanhedrin in importance. In the Minor Sanhedrins the greater part of Hebrew litigation was disposed of. The qualifications of the judges were similar to those for membership in the Great Sanhedrin.

The third order of courts among the Jews was known as The Lower Tribunal, or The Court of Three, because it had but three judges. These judges were chosen at the beginning of each case by the litigants themselves. The plaintiff chose one member, the defendant chose another, and these two selected the third. The court usually was held under a tree or at the city gate. These courts of three correspond to the court of the justice of the peace of our day. They had jurisdiction only in civil matters of small importance and in petty criminal offenses.

Organization of the Sanhedrin

Since Jesus was tried before the Great Sanhedrin, we shall devote our time mostly to the study of that tribunal. The word "Sanhedrin" means an assembly. It is a Hebrew-Aramaic word, indicating a legislative assembly or ecclesiastical council deliberating in a sitting posture. The Great Sanhedrin was composed of seventy members and a presiding officer, making seventy-one in all. It doubtless had its origin with Moses in the wilderness, when seventy of the princes of Israel were chosen as his counselors. See Numbers 11: 16, 17. The president of the Great Sanhedrin was styled the prince. There was also a vice-president, known as the father of the tribunal. This second officer presided in the absence of the president.

The president was usually the high priest, but not always. Gamaliel served in this capacity for twenty years and never held the office of high priest. Moses was president of the council of seventy, which was really the first Sanhedrin, at the same time that Aaron was the high priest. Maimonides declared that "whoever surpassed his colleagues in wisdom was made by them chief of the Sanhedrin."—*See Chandler, vol. 1, p. 113.* The seventy-one members sat in a semicircle, with the president occupying the central place. He thus had thirty-five members on each side of him. They all "sat, turbaned, on cushions or pillows, in

Oriental fashion, with crossed legs, and unshod feet, in a half circle."—"*The Life and Words of Christ*," *Geikie, page 746.* The high priest was distinguished from the other members of the Sanhedrin by his breastplate containing twelve precious stones, representing the twelve tribes of Israel; by his turban of blue inwrought with gold; and by his flowing blue robe with its girdle of purple, scarlet, and gold embroidery.

The minutes of the proceedings were kept by two secretaries, or scribes, who were doctors of the law. They sat directly in front of the presiding officer, in a position where they could hear the testimony of all. The one on the left recorded the accusations of the witnesses against the accused, together with the votes for condemnation and the reasons given by the voting judges. The scribe on the right recorded the testimony and the votes favoring acquittal. The accused stood in the center of the semicircle, where he could be seen and heard by all. Twenty-three of the seventy-one members constituted a quorum. A majority of two or more was necessary to convict, and a majority of one to acquit. Cases could be appealed from the Minor Sanhedrin to the Great Sanhedrin, whose decisions were final. " 'Its authority was supreme in all matters; civil and political, social, religious, and criminal.' "—"*The Trial of Jesus*," *Chandler, vol. 1, p. 120.*

The membership of the Great Sanhedrin was divided into three groups, or chambers. Originally there were twenty-three in each group, which, with the presiding officer and the vice-president, made up the seventy-one. The first of these groups was known as the Chamber of Priests, or the Chamber of High Priests, and was the first in importance. It was the sacerdotal order, and contained the former high priests, of which there were twelve living at the time of

Christ's trial. One of these was Annas. The high priest at the time of Jesus was elected each year, subject to the approval of the Roman procurator, the office usually going to the highest bidder. Others besides former high priests were members of this order.

The second group was the Chamber of Scribes, sometimes also called the College of Rabbis. It was the literary, or legal, order. Its members were the teachers and wise men, and were therefore called rabbis. It is claimed that Gamaliel belonged to this order, as did also Saul of Tarsus, Barnabas, and Stephen, three of his disciples. It is said that the term "rabbi" was first applied to Gamaliel. His greatness is indicated by the following statement from the Talmud: "With the death of Rabbi Gamaliel the glory of the law has departed." The following precepts recorded in the Talmud show the reverence demanded by the rabbis, and throw light on some of Christ's scathing rebukes of this order: "The honor due to a teacher borders on that due to God." "The sayings of the scribes were weightier than those of the law." "If anyone thinks evil of his rabbi, it is as if he thought evil of the Eternal." "If anyone quarrels with his rabbi, it is as if he contended with the living God." "If anyone opposes his rabbi, he is guilty in the same degree as if he opposed God Himself."—*See Chandler, vol. 2, p. 316.* Jesus refused to give the scribes the respect they demanded; therefore they hated and persecuted Him.

Qualifications for Membership

The third division of the Great Sanhedrin was the Chamber of Elders. This was the patriarchal order, and represented the popular and democratic element of the nation. To this class belonged Nicodemus and Joseph of

Arimathaea, the former being one of the three richest men in Jerusalem. The Talmud declares that "each of whom [the three] could have supported the whole city for ten years."—*See Chandler, vol. 2, p. 321.* Doras was another member of this order. He hired men to assassinate the high priest Jonathan in 52 or 53 A. D. The money was furnished by the Roman governor, Felix, because Jonathan had criticized his administration. Josephus and the Talmud give us the names and biographies of more than forty of the members of the Sanhedrin that condemned Jesus. Most of them were haughty, ambitious, overbearing, scheming priests, who believed themselves to be infallible. The three orders that composed the Sanhedrin are often mentioned in the New Testament. See Matthew 26: 57, 59; Mark 14: 43.

The qualifications for membership in the Great Sanhedrin, if strictly enforced, would make injustice impossible. The following are the most prominent membership requirements as listed in Hebrew literature: 1. To be eligible for membership in the supreme court of the Jews a man must be a Hebrew and a lineal descendant of Hebrew parents. Paul referred to this rule when he said he was "of the stock of Israel, of the tribe of Benjamin, an Hebrew of the Hebrews." Philippians 3: 5. 2. He must be "learned in the law," both oral and written. He must be well versed in both the Mishna and the Gemara, which together make up the Talmud. 3. He must have had judicial experience in at least three offices of gradually increasing dignity, beginning with a local court and including two Minor Sanhedrins in Jerusalem. 4. He must have a thorough knowledge of the known sciences of the time, including that of medicine. He must be versed in the principles of chemistry and physiology. It is recorded that Rabbi Ismael and his disciples dissected human bodies in order to become better acquainted with the physical structure of man. Eighty students of the Academy of Hillel are said to have become proficient in every branch of science known.

5. A member of the Sanhedrin must be an accomplished linguist, and be able to speak the languages of the surrounding nations. 6. He must be modest, popular, of good appearance, and free from haughtiness. 7. He must be pious, strong, and courageous. 8. He must have no physical blemishes, because he was a type of the Messiah. The Talmud lists one hundred forty bodily defects, any one of which would disqualify a man for the office. An examination was made to see that the candidate was free from all these blemishes.

9. The candidate for membership must have learned a trade, or occupation. Rabbi Jehuda declared that "he who does not teach his son a trade is much the same as if he taught him to be a thief." See Acts 18: 3.

10. Another rule was that he must be a married man, and have children of his own. They "must be married men, and fathers, as being more likely than others to be humane and considerate."—"*The Desire of Ages,*" *page 133.* This also throws light upon the much discussed question regarding Paul's family status. 11. And, finally, he must be over forty years of age. In Hebrew law a boy reached the years of accountability at twelve, became a man at twenty-five, a priest at thirty, and a counselor at forty.

This was the court, and these were the judges, before whom Jesus of Nazareth was tried and condemned on the charge of blasphemy. It was before this tribunal that He who had departed from evil made Himself a prey, "and the Lord saw it, and it displeased Him that there was no judgment." Isaiah 59: 14, 15.

CHAPTER NINE

LOFTY PRINCIPLES OF HEBREW LAW

It is appropriate that we here study briefly the principles of Hebrew law. The chief foundation of the laws of the ancient Hebrews was the Mosaic code embodied in the Pentateuch and referred to in the New Testament as "the law of Moses" and "the book of the law." Next in importance were the rabbinic interpretations of this code as contained in the Talmud. Walter M. Chandler declares that "the Pentateuch was the foundation, the cornerstone; the Talmud was the superstructure, the gilded dome of the great temple of Hebrew justice."—*"The Trial of Jesus," vol. 1, pp. 73, 74.* The word Talmud means "to teach," or "teaching," or "learning." Chandler says that the Talmud is "an encyclopedia of the life and literature, law and religion, art and science of the Hebrew people during a thousand years." Emanuel Deutsch, in his essay on the Talmud, says that it is "a Corpus Juris, an encyclopedia of law, civil and penal, ecclesiastical and international, human and divine."—*See Chandler, vol. 1, p. 74.*

Speaking of the size of the Talmud at the present time, a student of Hebrew law says: "Modern editions of the Talmud, including the most important commentaries, consist of about 3,000 folio sheets, or 12,000 folio pages of closely printed matter, generally divided into twelve or twenty volumes. One page of Talmudic Hebrew intelligibly translated into English would cover three pages; the translation of the whole Talmud with its commentaries would accordingly make a library of 400 volumes, each numbering 360 octavo pages."—*"The Criminal Jurisprudence of the*

Ancient Hebrews," Mendelsohn, page 189, note 1. (*Chandler.*) So comprehensive is this compilation of the rabbis that Philip Berger Benny calls it "the compendium of their literature, the storehouse of their tradition, the exponent of their faith, the record of their requirements, the handbook of their ceremonials and the summary of their legal code, civil and penal."—"*The Criminal Code of the Jews,*" (*Chandler.*)

The Jewish Talmud

The Talmud is divided into two parts. The first division is known as the Mishna, which means "Repetition." The Mishna is subdivided into six sections. It is a vast mass of tradition, or oral law, which was reduced to writing near the close of the second century of the Christian Era. It is sometimes described as the "text" of the Talmud. The second section of the Talmud is known as the Gemara, or "Commentary." It is the rabbinical exposition of the meaning of the Mishna. The relation between the Mishna and the Gemara may be compared to a bill introduced into a congress or parliament and the debate and discussions that follow. The Talmud is revered by the Jews as much or even more than are the Scriptures. "The Bible is salt, the Mishna pepper, the Gemara balmy spice," is a rabbinic adage. The Talmud is to the religion of the Jews what the traditions of the Fathers are to the Roman Catholic Church and its doctrines.

Hebrew law provided four methods of punishments for capital crimes. These were: beheading, strangling, burning, and stoning. The Pentateuch and the Talmud enumerate thirty-six capital offenses. Two were punished by beheading, six by strangling, ten by burning, and eighteen by stoning. Crucifixion was not a Jewish punishment. Beheading was accomplished by tying the culprit to a post and severing the head from the body with a sword. Strangling was effected by burying the victim to his waist in mud or soil, and then tightening a cord around his neck until he suffocated. Burning had no resemblance to the form of punishment used on "heretics" during the Middle Ages. A pit was dug in which the victim was made to stand, and then soil was thrown in and tamped down until only his head and shoulders remained above ground. A cord was then wrapped around his neck, and two strong men drew on the two ends until suffocation resulted. When the lower jaw dropped because of unconsciousness, a lighted wick was thrown into his mouth.

Safeguards of Justice

Stoning was accomplished by taking the criminal to the top of a rock or cliff, stripping him of his clothes, and throwing him with violence to the bottom. If this did not produce death, the witnesses to the crime threw heavy stones onto the body. If life still remained, the bystanders were permitted to cast stones till the victim was dead. "The hands of the witnesses shall be first upon him to put him to death, and afterward the hands of all the people. So thou shalt put the evil away from among you." Deuteronomy 17:7. This is the authority for the rule. This method of stoning throws light on the effort to put Christ to death at Nazareth when He claimed to be the Messiah, as recorded in Luke 4:28-30. Stoning was the penalty for blasphemy, and the record indicates an attempt to stone Jesus because of His claim to divinity.

No system of law in all human history so jealously and

sacredly guarded justice as did that of the Hebrews. "Where no counsel is, the people fall: but in the multitude of counselors there is safety." Proverbs 11: 14. An American lawyer wrote regarding this principle of Hebrew law: "No court, among the ancient Hebrews, could consist of a single judge. Three was the number of the lowest court; three and twenty, of the next highest; and seventy-one, of the Great Sanhedrin at Jerusalem. A single intelligence acting judicially would have been regarded as a usurpation of divine prerogative. The basis of this peculiar Hebrew notion is a single sentence from the Pirke Aboth, iv. 8: 'Be not a sole judge, for there is no sole judge but One.' "—"*The Trial of Jesus,*" *Chandler, vol. 1, p. 126.*

Hebrew jurisprudence provided no advocates either to defend or to prosecute. The judges were the defenders, and the witnesses the prosecutors. "The only *prosecutors* known to Talmudic criminal jurisprudence are the witnesses to the crime. Their duty is to bring the matter to the cognizance of the court, and to bear witness against the criminal. In capital cases, they are the legal executioners also. Of an official accuser or prosecutor there is nowhere any trace in the laws of the ancient Hebrews."—"*The Criminal Jurisprudence of the Ancient Hebrews,*" *Mendelsohn, page 110.* (Chandler.)

The Jews considered paid advocates as barriers to justice. In this opinion the Jews were not alone. Plato considered lawyers the plague of the community; and when King Ferdinand of Spain sent colonists to the West Indies, he gave instruction "that no lawyers should be carried along, lest lawsuits should become ordinary occurrences in the New World."—*Id., page 140.*

In Hebrew law, at least two witnesses were required to

bring conviction. The foundation for this rule is found in Deuteronomy 17: 6. "At the mouth of two witnesses, or three witnesses, shall he that is worthy of death be put to death; but at the mouth of one witness he shall not be put to death." See also Numbers 35: 30; Deuteronomy 19: 15. The testimony of the witnesses must agree in all essential details, or it was rejected. "If one witness contradicts another, the testimony is not accepted."—*Mishna*, "*Sanhedrin*," C. V. 2. Hebrew law did not permit any circumstantial evidence in a criminal case. "Hearsay evidence was barred equally in civil as in criminal cases, no matter how strongly the witness might believe in what he heard and however worthy and numerous were his informants."—"*The Martyrdom of Jesus*," *Rabbi Isaac M. Wise*. In a Hebrew court, witnesses were not required to take oath, because, "whosoever will not tell the truth without an oath, would not scruple to assert falsehood with an oath."—*Talmud*. This is logical, and is in harmony with the teachings of Jesus. Matthew 5: 33-37. (Chandler.)

Under Hebrew law false witnesses were very severely dealt with. Perjury placed a witness in a position as serious as that of the one he testified against. "Hebrew law provided that false witnesses should suffer the penalty provided for the commission of the crime which they sought by their testimony to fix upon the accused."—"*The Trial of Jesus*," *Chandler, vol. 1, p. 140*. This rule is based upon Deuteronomy 19: 18-21. Such a rule, if strictly enforced, would soon reduce perjury to a minimum. The application of the principle would also close the mouths of gossipers. "Every possible precaution was taken to render impossible the wrongful conviction of an accused person. The student of Hebrew law is at times astonished by the excessive caution inculcated in criminal procedure. . . . The judges leaned always to the side of the defendant and gave him the advantage of every possible doubt."—"*The Trial of Jesus,*" *Chandler, vol. 1, pp. 153, 154.*

And then, more effectively to safeguard justice, a series of maxims was prepared to guide the judges in their work: "A judge should always consider that a sword threatens him from above, and destruction yawns at his feet." "Be cautious and slow in judgment, send forth many disciples, and make a fence around the law." "When a judge decides not according to truth, he makes the majesty of God to depart from Israel. But if he judges according to the truth, were it only for one hour, it is as if he established the whole world, for it is in judgment that the divine presence in Israel has its habitation." These and many others recorded in the Talmud remind judges of their solemn duty and responsibility. Besides these maxims there were four fundamental rules of procedure in criminal cases that safeguarded justice—"strictness in the accusation, publicity in the discussion, full freedom granted to the accused, and assurance against all dangers or errors of testimony."—"*Histoire des Institutions de Moise,*" *Salvador.* Chandler, quoting this noted Jewish physician and lawyer, calls him "the Jewish Blackstone."

Sanctity of Human Life

In Hebrew jurisprudence every possible effort was made to save and to protect human life because it belonged to God. The Mishna declares that "the Sanhedrin which so often as once in seven years condemns a man to death, is a slaughterhouse." (Chandler.) Dr. R. Eliezer, to quote Greenleaf, says that the Sanhedrin "deserves this appellation when it pronounces a like sentence once in seventy years." Benny declares that it was a maxim of the Jews that "the Sanhedrin was to save, not to destroy life." (Chandler.) Other maxims recorded in the Mishna are: "Man's life belongs to God, and only according to the law of God may it be disposed of." "Whosoever preserves one worthy life is as meritorious as if he had preserved the world." To ensure justice to the accused the arguments must begin in his behalf. Nothing was permitted to be said against him till after at least one of the judges had spoken in his behalf.

In case of conviction in a capital trial, sentence could not be pronounced till the afternoon of the second day. After the first conviction, the judges left the hall of hewn stone and gathered in groups of five or six to discuss the case. They then walked home by twos, arm in arm, still seeking for arguments in behalf of the accused. After sunset they made calls on one another to discuss the case further, and to pray for divine guidance. The next day was supposed to be a day of prayer and fasting, nothing being eaten till the case was disposed of. After the morning sacrifice the judges reassembled and carefully reviewed the evidence. Judges were permitted to change their votes to favor the accused, but not to condemn him. The Sanhedrin deliberated all day till near sunset, when the final vote was taken. If the accused was again pronounced guilty, the witnesses led him forth to the execution while the Sanhedrin remained in session. A man was stationed at the door of the hall with a red banner, and another, mounted on a horse, followed the procession, he also having a red flag. The latter proclaimed to the gazing multitude that if anyone knew of any evidence in favor of the prisoner he should come forth and speak. If any responded with any new evidence, the procession was halted and the banner waved to announce to the guard at the door of the hall that the prisoner was being returned to the Sanhedrin for a new trial. Or if while the prisoner was being taken to the place of execution a person came to the hall and announced that he had fresh evidence in behalf of the accused, the man at the door waved his banner and the procession was halted, and the witnesses brought back their prisoner for a new hearing.

It was before a court with such marvelous maxims and rules to insure justice that a wrongful conviction was impossible, that Jesus, the Innocent One, was unjustly tried and condemned to die, that we who deserve nothing but death might be justified and given eternal life. "Christ was treated as we deserve, that we might be treated as He deserves. He was condemned for our sins, in which He had no share, that we might be justified by His righteousness, in which we had no share. He suffered the death which was ours, that we might receive the life which was His. 'With His stripes we are healed.' "—"*The Desire of Ages,*" *page 25.*

CHAPTER TEN

MOST NOTABLE TRIAL IN HISTORY

THE ANNALS of man record many notable criminal trials, of which the following are a few of the most famous: Socrates was tried and condemned to die by the court of Athens. He was accused of corrupting Athenian youth, blaspheming the Olympic gods, and undermining the constitution of the Attic Republic. The trial of Charles I of England was followed by his execution and the reign of Cromwell. Warren Hastings, the first English governor-general of India, was acquitted after a trial that lasted eight years. Aaron Burr was tried for treason in Richmond, Virginia, and was acquitted. The trial lasted six months, and it forms one of the darkest chapters in American history. The trial of Alfred Dreyfus and his banishment to Devil's Island is doubtless the most notable in the history of France. The trial and execution of Mary Stuart, the Scottish queen, by the consent of her cousin, Queen Elizabeth of England, ended a long and bitter rivalry over the throne of England, and forms a black chapter in British history. The criminal proceedings against Robert Emmet, Irish patriot, was also a notable trial.

These great criminal cases, however, become almost insignificant when compared with the trial and execution of Jesus of Nazareth. Salvador, a Jewish advocate, declares it to be "the most memorable trial in history." Regarding only one phase of this trial, Walter M. Chandler said: "Standing alone, the Hebrew trial of Christ would have been the most thrilling and impressive judicial proceeding in all history."—"*The Trial of Jesus,*" *vol. 2, p. 4.* Of the entire proceedings the same author wrote: "The trial of the Nazarene was before the high tribunals of both heaven and earth; before the Great Sanhedrin, whose judges were the master spirits of a divinely commissioned race; before the court of the Roman Empire that controlled the legal and political rights of men throughout the known world, from Scotland to Judea and from Dacia to Abyssinia."—*Id., Preface to Volume One, page xvi.* Jesus was tried and condemned by two separate tribunals, one Hebrew and the other Roman.

Testimony of History

Profane history furnishes a number of witnesses to the fact that Jesus lived in Judea and died on the cross. Flavius Josephus, the famous Jewish historian who lived near the time of Christ, wrote regarding Him: "Now there was about this time Jesus, a wise man, if it be lawful to call Him a man; for He was a doer of wonderful works. . . . And when Pilate, at the suggestion of the principal men amongst us, had condemned Him to the cross, those that loved Him at the first did not forsake Him. . . . And the tribe of Christians, so named from Him, are not extinct at this day."—*"Antiquities of the Jews," book 18, chap. 3, par. 3.* The genuineness of the second clause has long been questioned, but in recent years it is being more and more accepted as authentic. "I believe the passage respecting Jesus to be authentic."—*"The Life of Jesus," Renan, page 29.*

Tacitus, a Roman historian of the first century, wrote regarding the report that Nero had been responsible for the burning of Rome: "In order to quiet the report, Nero accused and punished with the most refined tortures those who with perverse obstinacy called themselves Christians. The author of this name was Christ, who under the reign of Tiberius was executed by the procurator Pontius Pilate."—"*Annals,*" *xv, 44.* Tacitus was the author of sixteen books called "Annals." Jesus is also mentioned by Suetonius, a Roman historian born about 68 A. D.; by Titus Livius, another Roman writer, who died in the first century of our era; by Philo Judæus, Jewish philosopher, who was a contemporary of Jesus; by Epictetus, Roman Stoic philosopher born in the middle of the first century; by Pliny the Younger, Roman author and soldier, who died about 114 A. D.; and by Lucian, a Greek author who lived about 120-200 A. D. There are also a few references to Jesus in the Talmud.

The principal witnesses to the life, teachings, trials, and crucifixion of Jesus are the four evangelists, Matthew, Mark, Luke, and John. Paul and the other New Testament writers have also given important testimony. But is the testimony of these men, some of whom claim to be eyewitnesses, dependable? Will the written testimony of these men, long since dead, stand the legal tests applied to witnesses in modern courts of law? The law of evidence, which regulates the testimony of witnesses in modern courts, involves two important questions: First, Is their testimony admissible as evidence? and second, Is it dependable or credible? Let us put the testimony of the disciples of Jesus to the legal test of the law of evidence.

The Law of Evidence

The greatest of all authorities on the law or rules of evidence is Simon Greenleaf, LL. D., late Professor of Law in Harvard University and the author of "Treatise on the Law of Evidence," which is recognized throughout the legal world as almost the last word on the subject. The *North American Review* declared Simon Greenleaf to be "a writer of the highest authority on legal subjects, whose life has been spent in weighing testimony and sifting evidence, and whose published opinions on the rules of evidence are received as authoritative in all the English and American tribunals." The London *Law Magazine* said regarding this great American lawyer: "It is no mean honor to America that her schools of jurisprudence have produced two of the first writers and best esteemed legal authorities of this century—the great and good man, Judge Story, and his worthy and eminent associate, Professor Greenleaf. Upon the existing 'Law of Evidence' (by Greenleaf), more light has shone from the New World than from all the lawyers who adorn the courts of Europe." These two statements show the legal standing of the man whose testimony we shall take regarding the credibility of the Gospel writers as witnesses to the trial and crucifixion of Jesus.

In 1903, Simon Greenleaf published a book entitled "The Testimony of the Evangelists Examined by the Rules of Evidence Administered in Courts of Justice." In this book the noted jurist puts the scriptural record to the legal tests, and declares it to be admissible and dependable evidence. He wrote: "Every document, apparently ancient, coming from the proper repository or custody, and bearing on its face no evident marks of forgery, the law presumes to be genuine, and devolves on the opposing party the burden of proving it to be otherwise. . . . The burden of showing them [ancient documents] to be false and unworthy of credit, is devolved on the party who makes that objection. The presumption of law is the judgment of charity. It presumes that every man is innocent until he is proved guilty; that everything has been done fairly and legally, until it is proved to have been otherwise; and that every document, found in its proper repository, and not bearing marks of forgery, is genuine."—*Pages 7, 8.*

In applying this argument to the credibility of the four Gospels, Greenleaf says: "If any ancient document concerning our public rights were lost, copies which had been as universally received and acted upon as the four Gospels have been, would have been received in evidence in any of our courts of justice, without the slightest hesitation. The entire text of the Corpus Juris Civilis is received as authority in all the courts of Continental Europe, upon much weaker evidence of its genuineness; for the integrity of the Sacred Text has been preserved by the jealousy of opposing sects, beyond any moral possibility of corruption. . . . It is quite erroneous to suppose that the Christian is bound to offer any further proof of their genuineness or authenticity. It is for the objector to show them spurious; for on him, by the plainest rules of law, lies the burden of proof."—*Id., pages 9, 10.*

The Rule for Credible Testimony

Greenleaf lays down the following rule as to credible testimony: "In the absence of circumstances which generate suspicion, every witness is to be presumed credible, until the contrary is shown; the burden of impeaching his credibility lying on the objector." The writer then applies this well-established rule of evidence to the testimony of the Gospel witnesses: "This rule serves to show the injustice with which the writers of the Gospels have ever been treated by infidels; an injustice silently acquiesced in even by Christians; in requiring the Christian affirmatively, and by positive evidence . . . to establish the credibility of his witnesses above all others, before their testimony is entitled to be considered, and in permitting the testimony of a single profane writer, alone and uncorroborated, to outweigh that of any single Christian. . . . It is time that this injustice should cease; that the testimony of the evangelists should be admitted to be true, until it can be disproved by those who would impugn it; that the silence of one sacred writer on any point, should no more detract from his own veracity or that of the other historians, than the like circumstance is permitted to do among profane writers; and that the four evangelists should be admitted in corroboration of each other, as readily as Josephus and Tacitus, or Polybius and Livy."—*Id., pages 25, 26.*

Here are statements regarding the principles of the law of evidence that are of inestimable value to Christians in dealing with their opponents. Many become greatly concerned over the safety of their religion and the foundations of their faith because they are not able to produce all the evidence demanded by some boasting infidel or sneering skeptic. There are many questions in every realm of life and sphere of thought that no person can answer to the satisfaction of the questioner or even of himself. Asking questions is always easier than answering them; and the Christian can ask the skeptic more puzzling questions than the skeptic can ask the Christian. The Christian has the right at least to demand that he ask every other question. But according to the well-established rules of evidence recognized in every court in the world, the Christian does not need to answer any of the skeptics' questions regarding the credibility of the Scriptures, because they would be accepted as reliable testimony, and, if their authority were questioned, the burden of proof would be thrown back upon the objector. It is the duty of the critic to prove his criticism, rather than that of the Christian to answer it. If this principle were applied, it would save the church and its ministers a vast amount of time and expense now consumed in answering caviling skeptics, so that their talents and energies could be employed in the more profitable work of proclaiming a positive message of salvation from sin. Jesus said: "If ye continue in My word, then are ye My disciples indeed; and ye shall know the truth, and the truth shall make you free." John 8: 31, 32.

CHAPTER ELEVEN

CREDIBILITY OF THE GOSPEL WITNESSES

CAN WE depend on the written accounts of the four Gospel writers in regard to the trials and crucifixion of Jesus? Before considering the most notable trial and execution in human history, let us consider from a legal standpoint the credibility of the four Gospel witnesses. Greenleaf gives the following five tests of credibility: "The credit due to the testimony of witnesses depends upon, firstly, their honesty; secondly, their ability; thirdly, their number and the consistency of their testimony; fourthly, the conformity of their testimony with experience; and fifthly, the coincidence of their testimony with collateral circumstances."—*"The Testimony of the Evangelists," page 28.* He then tries the four Gospel writers by these legal tests, and abundantly proves that they are dependable and credible witnesses.

Let us apply these five tests to the disciples of Jesus. In the first place, were they honest and sincere? Did they intend to tell the truth? Did they believe their own testimony? If these questions can be answered in the affirmative, the four evangelists were honest witnesses. The test of sincerity involves two things—namely, character and motive. Perfect sincerity is produced only by righteous characters and honest motives. If the writers were good men, they believed what they taught and wrote, and were therefore sincere. Good men could never have palmed off on the world an impostor. Their writings would be a forgery if they were not true, and the writers would therefore be guilty of perjury. If they were bad men, their writings and teachings would furnish abundance of proof. None but noble characters could have painted such a character as that of the Christ, "the realized ideal of humanity." If the disciples were insincere, what motive prompted them to preach their message and finally to die for it? All of them, except John, suffered martyrdom for their faith. It is impossible to think that they were seeking earthly rewards, for Jesus had promised them persecution "even unto death." Their very teaching arrayed against them every earthly power. Jesus had promised them a future reward in a future life. Matthew 23:34; 19:27, 28. Since their motives were to gain a heavenly reward, they must have been honest and sincere men, and any court would so decide.

Test of Ability to Testify

The second test is the ability to testify. This depends on two considerations. The first is the natural powers of observation and the strength of memory. A witness, in order to be permitted to testify, must have a sound mind and have average intelligence. Greenleaf says: "It is always to be presumed that men are honest, and of sound mind, and of the average and ordinary degree of intelligence. This is not the judgment of mere charity; it is also the uniform presumption of the law of the land; a presumption which is always allowed freely and fully to operate, until the fact is shown to be otherwise."—*Id., pages 31, 32.* No one can honestly question the intellectual ability of the four evangelists to observe and remember that of which they bear witness. Matthew was a publican, or taxgatherer, and thus an official for the Romans, before he became a follower of Christ. His book is thought to have been written six years after the events occurred. Luke was a physician, which would indicate more than average intelligence. His book is said to have been written twenty-eight years after Christ ascended. The writings of all four give evidence of intelligence and scholarship of a high order. Three of the Gospels were written in Greek, a foreign tongue, and the other in Hebrew. Their writings are classics in both language and construction as well as in beauty of expression.

The ability to testify also depends upon the opportunities a witness has to observe the things about which he testifies. Two, if not three, of the evangelists were eyewitnesses. John Mark was doubtless personally acquainted with Jesus. It is believed that he was the young man mentioned by himself as being in the Garden of Gethsemane when Jesus was arrested. Mark 14: 51, 52. Some Bible students have advanced the thought that Peter was the real author of the second of the Gospels, having dictated it to Mark. In either case, the writer spoke from experience and observation. Also, the relating of their own blunders gives force to the presumption of truthfulness. The writers often place themselves in a very unfavorable light. They tell how they all slept while Jesus prayed, and all fled when He was arrested. Peter's base denial is faithfully recorded. Such recitals would have been eliminated from the narrative if written by designing and dishonest men, who would have made heroes of themselves.

Critics sometimes contend that the testimony of the disciples is unreliable because they wrote of their own Lord and Master. This is unsound and unreasonable argument. Such a rule, if applied to secular literature, would exclude "Recollections of Socrates," because it was written by Xenophon, the disciple and friend of Socrates; Boswell's "Life of Johnson," because it was written by a friend and admirer; and the "Commentaries of Cæsar," because they were written by Cæsar himself. The same can be said of almost all biographies. In fact, such reasoning would delete from our libraries a large portion of the books that are accepted without question. In their anxiety to destroy the testimony of Scripture, skeptics nullify their own arguments.

Test of Witnesses

The third test of credibility is the number of witnesses and the consistency of their testimony. The testimony of a witness is greatly strengthened by other witnesses who tell virtually the same story. The greater the number of supporting witnesses the more reliable the testimony is considered to be. Courts of law do not consider omissions as contradictions, nor should we. "An investigation of the charge of discrepancy against the Gospel writers shows that the critics and skeptics have classified mere *omissions* as contradictions. Nothing could be more absurd than to consider an omission a contradiction, unless the requirements of the case show that the facts and circumstances omitted were essential to be stated, or that the omission was evidently intended to mislead or deceive. Any other contention would turn historical literature topsy-turvy and load it down with contradictions."—"*The Trial of Jesus,*" *Chandler, vol. 1, p. 30.*

This criticism of the skeptics is likewise destroyed by numberless examples from secular literature. Dion Cassius, Tacitus, and Suetonius, all wrote histories covering the reign of Tiberius. Each of these writers mentions many things omitted by the others. Does this give rise to the presumption of fraud and make it necessary to reject all three as unreliable? Also Abbott, Hazlitt, and Walter Scott wrote biographies of Napoleon Bonaparte, and no one of them related all the events recorded by the other two. Do these omissions affect the credibility of any of these writers? "The opponents of Christianity are never embarrassed in excusing or explaining away omissions or contradictions, provided the writer is a layman and his subject secular. But let the theme be a sacred one, and the author an ecclesiastic—preacher, priest, or prophet—and immediately incredulity rises to high tide, engulfs the reason, and destroys all dispassionate criticism."—*Id., page 31.* Again the critics go so far that they destroy their own reasoning.

Testing the Testimony

When a number of witnesses say the same thing in the same way and in the same terms, it always increases the suspicion of fraud or conspiracy. The four evangelists wrote at different times and in different places, and their very omissions and apparent contradictions or inconsistencies prove that there was no fraud or conspiracy on their part. Conspirators would have fabricated exactly the same story, and related it in substantially the same language. "When accounts of a transaction come from the mouths of different witnesses, it is seldom that it is not possible to pick out apparent or real inconsistencies between them. These inconsistencies are studiously displayed by an adverse pleader, but oftentimes with little impression upon the minds of the judges. On the contrary, a close and minute agreement induces the suspicion of confederacy and fraud." —"*Evidences of Christianity,*" *William Paley, page 319. (Chandler.)*

The fourth test of credibility is the conformity of the testimony of witnesses with experience. The testimony of a witness must conform to the general experience of humanity at the time and in the place where the events occurred, it must agree with the history and customs of the times in that locality. For example, if a story of Benjamin Franklin should describe the use of telephones, radios, and railroads as being in use in colonial days, the entire book would be discredited. The skeptics declare that the miracles of Christ were not in conformity with human experience because they are contrary to the orderly course of natural law and the investigations of science. The skeptic Spinoza argued that miracles are impossible because "a miracle was *that*, the cause of which cannot be explained by our natural understanding from the known principles of natural things." (Chandler.) In answer to this argument, Greenleaf wrote: "Spinoza's argument against the possibility of miracles, was founded on the broad and bold assumption that all things are governed by immutable laws, or fixed modes of motion and relation, termed the laws of nature, by which God Himself is of necessity bound. This erroneous assumption is the tortoise, on which stands the elephant which upholds his system of atheism."—"*The Testimony of the Evangelists*," *page 36.* Spinoza's definition would place in the realm of miracles all freaks of nature, such as monstrosities, which cannot possibly be explained on the basis of natural law, and yet are known to be indisputable facts.

The fifth and last test of credibility is the coincidence of the testimony with collateral circumstances. The testimony of a witness must be in harmony with collateral and contemporaneous facts and circumstances if it is to be considered reliable. This is the chief test of credibility when the witness is dead or insane or absent, and only his writings are available, as in the case under consideration. The question is, Does the testimony agree with contemporary writers and the history of the times? On this point the great legal authority on evidence, Greenleaf, says: "This test is much more accurate than may at first be supposed. Every event which actually transpires, has its appropriate relation and place in the vast complication of circumstances, of which the affairs of men consist; it owes its origin to the events which have preceded it, is intimately connected with all others which occur at the same time and place, and often with those of remote regions, and in its turn gives birth to numberless others which succeed. In all this almost inconceivable contexture, and seeming discord, there is perfect harmony; and while the fact, which happened, tallies exactly with every other contemporaneous incident, related to it in the remotest degree, it is not possible for the wit of man to invent a story, which, if closely compared with the actual occurrences of the same time and place, may not be shown to be false."—*Id., page 43.* See also "Starkie on Evidence," pages 496-499.

They Fail

Under this acid test of reliability all novels fail in truthfulness, and on this basis the apocryphal books were eliminated from the canon of Scripture. Tested by these same fundamental principles, the testimony of the evangelists and of all the sacred writers stands unimpeached and unshaken. The Scriptures are in perfect accord with the testimony of contemporary writers and of the discoveries of science. The light being shed on the ancient world by the discoveries of archæology is corroborating the Scriptures to a remarkable degree. The evidences of the conformity of the writings of the four Gospel witnesses with contemporary writers will be considered as we discuss the events which occurred. Greenleaf said: "It is worthy of remark, that of all the investigations and discoveries of travelers and men of letters, since the overthrow of the Roman Empire, not a vestige of antiquity has been found, impeaching, in the slightest degree, the credibility of the sacred writers; but, on the contrary, every result has tended to confirm it."—"*The Testimony of the Evangelists,*" *page 47.* Chandler declares that "not only are the Gospels not contradicted by contemporaneous writers; they are also not impeached or disproved by later scientific research and historical investigation."—"*The Trial of Jesus,*" *vol. 1, p. 55.* With these facts and principles before us, we are ready to consider the New Testament record of the trial and crucifixion of Jesus of Nazareth.

CHAPTER TWELVE

JESUS BEFORE THE SANHEDRIN

"THEY led Jesus away to the high priest: and with him were assembled all the chief priests and the elders and the scribes." "And straightway in the morning the chief priests held a consultation with the elders and scribes and the whole council, and bound Jesus, and carried Him away, and delivered Him to Pilate." Mark 14: 53; 15: 1.

Hebrew law demanded two sessions of the Sanhedrin in case of condemnation, a day apart. Not until the afternoon of the second day could the final decree of death go forth, and the sentence be executed. It is evident from the above and other passages that there were two separate sessions of the Sanhedrin on the night of Christ's condemnation. The first was held very early in the morning before daylight, with only a portion of the members present, probably a quorum composed of the bitterest enemies of Jesus. With Caiaphas they had remained up all night in their anxiety to dispose of the Nazarene. The second session was held at break of day with "the elders and scribes and the whole council" present. Doubtless the morning meeting was an attempt to give a semblance of regularity and legality to the proceedings to make them conform to the rules of Hebrew law requiring at least two trials. These, however, were both held on the same day and only a few hours apart; they were, therefore, a mere subterfuge. When we consider the recklessness with which the judges of Jesus trampled underfoot the rules of Hebrew law, it is doubtful that they were even concerned about legality of procedure.

During the interval of one or two hours between the two

sessions of the Sanhedrin, Jesus was turned over to the mob to be tormented and persecuted. Mark 14:65; Luke 22:63-65. Spitting on another was regarded by the Jews as an expression of the greatest contempt. The awful treatment of Jesus as described by the Gospel writers was a fulfillment of prophecies concerning the Messiah: "The sorrows of death compassed Me, and the floods of ungodly men made Me afraid." "They that sit in the gate speak against Me; and I was the song of the drunkards." Psalms 18:4; 69:12. "I gave My back to the smiters, and My cheeks to them that plucked off the hair: I hid not My face from shame and spitting." Isaiah 50:6. "To them that jerked at My whiskers," is the Swedish translation. James Moffatt renders the passage: "I let them lash My back, and pluck My beard out: I never hid My face from shame and insult."

Two Distinct Charges

The imagination is incapable of picturing the awful scene of insult and torture that took place when Jesus was given into the hands of the rabble composed of cruel and unprincipled men. The laws of most nations presume a person to be innocent until he is proved guilty, and, until the final sentence of condemnation is passed, he is entitled to every possible protection from ill treatment. This cruel treatment of Jesus before He was legally tried and condemned was a base infraction of Hebrew law.

According to Mark 14:55-64, two separate charges were preferred against Jesus before the Hebrew tribunal. The first charge was sedition, which is "a rousing of discontent against government and disturbance of public tranquillity as by inflammatory speeches, etc."—*Webster*. Jesus was charged with the crime of speaking against the temple. He was also accused of denouncing cities, condemning the rich, defaming the scribes and Pharisees, subverting the laws and institutions of Moses, interfering with the services of the temple, and associating with the hated publicans. They declared that His teachings were undermining the authority of the priests over the people, and therefore breaking down the respect of the people for their spiritual leaders. We are told that the charge of sedition failed, and had to be abandoned because the witnesses "agreed not together." The testimony against Jesus was so manifestly contradictory and false that it had to be rejected.

The only hope of the enemies of Jesus to bring about His condemnation was a change of charges from sedition to blasphemy. The government of the Hebrews was considered a theocracy, with Jehovah as its real king and ruler. For this reason, blasphemy was considered a form of treason, with death by stoning as the penalty. It was one of the most serious offenses known to the Jews. Salvador, the Jewish advocate, said: "The senate declared that Jesus, son of Joseph, born at Bethlehem, had profaned the name of God in usurping it for Himself, a simple citizen. The capital sentence was then pronounced." (Chandler.) Jesus admitted the charge that He claimed to be the Son of God, or the Messiah, to be true, and on this confession He was condemned to die.

Beginning with His arrest in the Garden of Gethsemane, and ending with the sentence of death by the Great Sanhedrin, the entire proceedings against Jesus were illegal on more than a score of different counts. There were three infractions of Hebrew law in connection with His arrest, and four more during the preliminary hearings before Annas and Caiaphas. There was another when Jesus was turned over to be persecuted and tormented by the rabble before His final trial and condemnation. We have considered eight illegalities thus far, and shall attempt to deal with the others in the order in which they occurred.

The accusation or indictment was illegal because it was twofold—vague and indefinite. Salvador declared that "the entire criminal procedure of the Mosaic code rests upon four rules: certainty in the indictment; publicity in the discussion; full freedom granted to the accused; and assurance against all dangers or errors of testimony."—"*Histoire des Institutions de Moise,*" *Salvador, page 365.* (*Chandler.*) An indictment against a person must deal with a definite crime, and the trial must be carried to completion on the basis of that charge. No prosecutor is permitted to change charges during the proceedings because of his failure to prove those on which the indictment was based. When the false witnesses failed to prove the charge of sedition, Jesus should have been set at liberty and the case dismissed. But, instead, the presiding judge suddenly shifted to a new charge, that of blasphemy.

"The chief priests and all the council sought for witness against Jesus to put Him to death; and found none. For many bare false witness against Him, but their witness agreed not together. And there arose certain, and bare false witness against Him, saying, We heard Him say, I will destroy this temple that is made with hands, and within three days I will build another made without hands. But neither so did their witness agree together. And the high priest stood up in the midst, and asked Jesus, saying, Answerest Thou nothing? what is it which these witness against Thee? But He held His peace, and answered nothing." Mark 14: 55-61.

The use of false witnesses was a very grievous infraction

of Hebrew law. It not only disqualified a judge, who was supposed to seek for evidence only in behalf of the accused, but it also condemned the false witnesses to suffer the penalty they sought to bring upon the accused. Those who testified falsely against Jesus were therefore themselves deserving of death. For some time before His trial, the Jewish authorities had Jesus constantly shadowed by hired informers, or spies, which was entirely unlawful. "They watched Him, and sent forth spies, which should feign themselves just men, that they might take hold of His words, that so they might deliver Him unto the power and authority of the governor." Luke 20: 20. It was these paid spies who were brought forward to testify against Jesus, and whose testimony was too contradictory to effect a conviction. This failure caused Caiaphas to change the charge to that of blasphemy.

"But Jesus held His peace. And the high priest answered and said unto Him, I adjure Thee by the living God, that Thou tell us whether Thou be the Christ, the Son of God. Jesus saith unto him, Thou hast said: nevertheless I say unto you, Hereafter shall ye see the Son of man sitting on the right hand of power, and coming in the clouds of heaven. Then the high priest rent his clothes, saying, He hath spoken blasphemy; what further need have we of witnesses? behold, now ye have heard His blasphemy. What think ye? They answered and said, He is guilty of death." Matthew 26: 63-66.

Under Hebrew law the judges could not originate or prefer charges, nor could they prosecute the accused. The judges were the defenders, and only the witnesses could make the charges and testify against the defendant. "The Sanhedrin did not, and could not, originate charges; it only investigated those brought before it."—"*The Life and Times of Jesus the Messiah,*" *Alfred Edersheim, vol. 1, p. 309.* Edersheim was a Christian Jewish scholar of Vienna. A. Taylor Innes, a Scottish historian and lawyer of the eighteenth century, said: "The evidence of the leading witnesses constituted the charge. There was no other charge; no more formal indictment. Until they spoke, and spoke in the public assembly, the prisoner was scarcely an accused man. When they spoke, and the evidence of the two agreed together, it formed the legal charge, libel, or indictment, as well as the evidence for its truth."—"*The Trial of Jesus Christ,*" *page 41. (Chandler.)*

Regarding this point another legal authority says: "The only prosecutors known to Talmudic criminal jurisprudence are the witnesses to the crime. Their duty is to bring the matter to the cognizance of the court, and to bear witness against the criminal. In capital cases, they are the legal executioners also. Of an official accuser or prosecutor there is nowhere any trace in the laws of the ancient Hebrews." —"*The Criminal Jurisprudence of the Ancient Hebrews,*" *Mendelsohn, page 110. (Chandler.)*

Like the Romans, the Jews prohibited all legal proceedings by night. The chief reason given for this rule was that night trials would encourage secret sessions, which were forbidden. Justice has always demanded public hearings for the accused in order to avoid conspiracy. Of this rule of the Hebrew law, Mendelsohn said: "Criminal cases can be acted upon by the various courts during daytime only, by the Lesser Synhedrions from the close of the morning service till noon, and by the Great Synhedrion till evening." —*Id., page 112.* "Let a capital offense be tried during the day, but suspend it at night," is a statement in the Mishna.

"The reason why the trial of a capital offense could not be held at night is because, as oral tradition says, the examination of such a charge is like the diagnosing of a wound—in either case a more thorough and searching examination can be made by daylight."—*Maimonides, "Sanhedrin," III. (Chandler.)*

The Hebrew trial and condemnation of Jesus was illegal because it took place before the morning sacrifice. "The Sanhedrin sat from the close of the morning sacrifice to the time of the evening sacrifice."—*Talmud, Jerus., "Sanhedrin," C. I, fol. 19.* "No session of court could take place before the offering of the morning sacrifice."—*"Jesus Before the Sanhedrin," MM. Lemann, page 109.* "Since the morning sacrifice was offered at the dawn of day, it was hardly possible for the Sanhedrin to assemble until the hour after that time."—*Mishna, "Tamid, or of the Perpetual Sacrifice," C. III. (Chandler.)* The reason for this rule of Hebrew law was that no man was considered competent to act as a judge till after sacrifice and prayers had been offered to the great Judge of heaven. It also made impossible any night proceedings. The Hebrew trials of Jesus were entirely over soon after break of day, and hence before the morning sacrifice.

Hebrew law demanded two trials in case of conviction, covering two different days. The Hebrew trial of Jesus was illegal in that it was concluded within one day, the entire proceedings taking place the fourteenth of Nisan, the first lunar month, Hebrew time. The law on this point is stated in the Mishna as follows: "In pecuniary cases a trial may end the same day it began. In capital cases acquittal may be pronounced the same day, but the pronouncing of sentence of death must be deferred until the following day in the hope that some argument may meanwhile be discovered in favor of the accused."—*Mishna, n, 8; "Sanhedrin," 32.* "A criminal case resulting in the acquittal of the accused may terminate the same day on which the trial began. But if a sentence of death is to be pronounced, it cannot be concluded before the following day."—*Mishna, "Sanhedrin," IV, 1.*

The trial of Jesus was also illegal because it was held on the day preceding the Sabbath. Hebrew courts were not permitted to meet on the weekly Sabbath or on a festival sabbath. One reason was that the law did not permit writing on the Sabbath or on any holy day, and no court could do business without the recording of the proceedings by the scribes. "Court must not be held on the Sabbath, or on any holy day"—is the Talmudic law. For this reason the trial of a capital case could not be commenced on the day before the Sabbath because in case of conviction there must be a second trial the following day. "They shall not judge on the eve of the Sabbath, nor on that of any festival."—*Mishna, "Sanhedrin," IV, 1.* "No court of justice in Israel was permitted to hold sessions on the Sabbath or any of the seven Biblical holidays. In cases of capital crime, no trial could be commenced on Friday or the day previous to any holiday, because it was not lawful either to adjourn such cases longer than overnight, or to continue them on the Sabbath or holiday."—*"The Martyrdom of Jesus," Wise, page 67. (Chandler.)* The trial and execution of Jesus was not only on the day of the "preparation" of the weekly Sabbath, but also the day preceding the Passover sabbath. Because the Passover sabbath and the seventh-day Sabbath came together, that day was called "an high day." John 19: 31. In a double sense the proceedings against Jesus were illegal.

CHAPTER THIRTEEN

THE BREAKDOWN OF JUSTICE

LET US consider further points of illegality in the trial of Jesus before the supreme court of the Jews, showing the complete breakdown of justice in fulfillment of Isaiah 59: 14-16. The sentence against Jesus was unlawful because it was founded on His own confession. "Again the high priest asked Him, and said unto Him, Art Thou the Christ, the Son of the Blessed? And Jesus said, I am: and ye shall see the Son of man sitting on the right hand of power, and coming in the clouds of heaven. Then the high priest rent his clothes, and saith, What need we any further witnesses? Ye have heard the blasphemy: what think ye? And they all condemned Him to be guilty of death." Mark 14: 61-64.

Regarding the principles of Hebrew law on this point, Rabbi Wise said: "Self-accusation in cases of capital crime was worthless. For if not guilty he accuses himself of a falsehood; if guilty he is a wicked man, and no wicked man, according to Hebrew law, is permitted to testify, especially not in penal cases."—"*The Martyrdom of Jesus*," *page* 74. (*Chandler.*) The judges of Christ not only violated the law by taking the place of the witnesses as accusers, but also in extracting a confession from Jesus and then using it against Him. "We hold it as fundamental, that no one shall prejudice himself. If a man accuses himself before a tribunal, we must not believe him, unless the fact is attested by two other witnesses; and it is proper to remark, that the punishment of death inflicted upon Achan, in the time of Joshua, was an exception, occasioned by the nature of the circumstances; for our law does not condemn upon the simple confession of the accused, nor upon the declaration of one prophet alone." —*Hebrew law, quoted in "The Trial of Jesus Before Caiaphas and Pilate," Dupin.*

This rule of Hebrew law is further stated by Jewish writers: "We have it as a fundamental principle of our jurisprudence that no one can bring an accusation against himself. Should a man make confession of guilt before a legally constituted tribunal, such confession is not to be used against him unless properly attested by two other witnesses."—*Maimonides, "Sanhedrin," IV, 2.* "Not only is self-condemnation never extorted from the defendant by means of torture, but no attempt is ever made to lead him on to self-incrimination. Moreover, a voluntary confession on his part is not admitted in evidence, and therefore not competent to convict him, unless a legal number of witnesses minutely corroborate his self-accusation."—*"The Criminal Jurisprudence of the Ancient Hebrews," Mendelsohn, page 133. (Chandler.)* The reason for this rule is that frequently, in all parts of the world, many innocent persons confess crimes with which they had nothing to do. The Hebrew rule protected from self-incrimination.

A Strange Rule

One of the strangest rules of law ever known was the provision in Hebrew law that a person could not be convicted on a unanimous vote of the judges. "A simultaneous and unanimous verdict of guilt rendered on the day of the trial has the effect of an acquittal."—*Id., page 141.* Rabbi Wise said: "If none of the judges defend the culprit, i.e., all pronounce him guilty, having no defender in the court, the verdict of guilty was invalid and the sentence of death could not be executed."—*"The Martyrdom of Jesus," page 74.*

This rule prevailed because Hebrew law did not permit any defense advocates. It was the duty of the judges to defend the accused and to see that he received justice. In order to give the proceedings the proper element of mercy, the accused must have at least one friend among the judges to speak in his behalf.

Regarding this unusual rule, Chandler said: "With the Anglo-Saxon jury a unanimous verdict is necessary to convict, but with the Hebrew Sanhedrin unanimity was fatal, and resulted in an acquittal. . . . Now if the verdict was unanimous in favor of condemnation it was evident that the prisoner had had no friend or defender in court. To the Jewish mind this was almost equivalent to mob violence. It argued conspiracy, at least. The element of mercy, which was required to enter into every Hebrew verdict, was absent in such a case. . . . 'But where all suddenly agree on conviction, does it not seem,' asks a modern Jewish writer, 'that the convict is a victim of conspiracy and that the verdict is not the result of sober reason and calm deliberation?' . . . If the accused had one friend in court, the verdict of condemnation would stand, since the element of mercy was present and the spirit of conspiracy or mob violence was absent."—"*The Trial of Jesus,*" *vol. 1, pp. 280, 281.*

That Jesus was condemned by a unanimous vote of the Sanhedrin is evident from the scriptural record. As the result of the confession of Jesus that He was the Son of God, Caiaphas told the judges that they had heard His blasphemy. He then asked for their verdict. "They answered and said, He is guilty of death." "They all condemned Him to be guilty of death." Matthew 26:66; Mark 14:64. Rabbi Wise acknowledges that the sentence against Jesus rested on a unanimous verdict of the judges. That Jesus had no intercessor to defend Him is also evident from prophecy: "He saw that there was no man, and wondered that there was no intercessor: therefore His arm brought salvation unto Him; and His righteousness, it sustained Him." "I have trodden the wine press alone; and of the people there was none with Me." "And I looked, and there was none to help; and I wondered that there was none to uphold: therefore Mine own arm brought salvation unto Me; and My fury, it upheld Me." Isaiah 59: 16; 63: 3, 5. Jesus suffered the grossest injustice before the earthly tribunal without an intercessor that we might receive justice in the heavenly tribunal with Him as our intercessor.

In the light of human experience, the conduct of Jesus before the Sanhedrin was indeed strange. This is because it was divine. He held His peace when falsely accused, and spoke at a time when silence would have been a defense. On this point the noted Italian advocate said: "The condemnation had already been decided upon before the trial. . . . Jesus knew it, and disdained to reply to what was advanced in the first place because it was false; what was advanced in the second place He of His own accord and freely admitted, because in its material basis it was true. When a false and unjust charge was brought against Him, He held His peace, and He answered when no proof, not even a false one, constrained Him to speak. Novel and sublime behavior this, indeed, on the part of a prisoner at the bar." —*"The Trial of Jesus," Rosadi, page 180.*

To remain silent to the direct question as to whether He was the Messiah would have been to the decided personal advantage of Jesus. He would also have been within His legal rights, as no accused person was compelled to say or to do anything that would be prejudicial to his case.

But silence on this occasion would virtually have been a denial of His identity and mission. Likewise, silence on our part under some circumstances is a denial of Christ. An open and verbal denial such as Peter's is not the only way to betray our Lord.

Further Irregularities

The rending of his priestly robes not only disqualified Caiaphas to act as a judge; it brought upon his own head the very sentence that he was seeking to impose upon Jesus. The Mosaic code did not permit a high priest to "uncover his head;" and if he should rend his sacred priestly garments, the penalty was death. Leviticus 10: 6; 21: 10. The official garment of the high priest was not only symbolic of his sacred office in which he was the type of the Messiah, but his garments also represented the imputed and imparted righteousness of the Son of God. Such an act was also the evidence of a rage that was beneath the dignity of the high priest. In this effort to show his horror and indignation because of the confession of Jesus, Caiaphas pronounced himself guilty of death, and thus wholly disqualified himself to preside over the Sanhedrin. "An ordinary Israelite could, as an emblem of bereavement, tear his garments, but to the high priest it was forbidden, because his vestments, being made after the express orders of God, were figurative of his office."—*"Jesus Before the Sanhedrin," Lemann, page 140. (Chandler.)*

The balloting that condemned Jesus was also irregular. According to Hebrew law, in a criminal case the judges must vote one at a time, beginning with the youngest. Each in his turn had to arise and cast his vote and then state his reason for his decision. Both the vote and the reasons for it must be recorded by the scribes. That Jesus was condemned by acclamation is evident from Matthew 26: 66 and Mark 14: 64. An authority on Hebrew law says: "In ordinary cases the judges voted according to seniority, the oldest commencing; in a capital trial, the reverse order was followed. That the younger members of the Sanhedrin should not be influenced by the views or arguments of their more mature, more experienced colleagues, the junior judge was in these cases always the first to pronounce for or against a conviction."—*"The Criminal Code of the Jews," Benny, pages 73, 74. (Chandler.)*

Jewish writers have also stated this law in such clear terms as to leave no doubt as to what course should have been followed at the trial of Jesus: "Let the judges each in his turn absolve or condemn."—*Mishna, "Sanhedrin," XV, 5.* It was only by this means of voting that the decisions of the various judges could be recorded by the scribes. "The members of the Sanhedrin were seated in the form of a semicircle at the extremity of which a secretary was placed, whose business it was to record the votes. One of these secretaries recorded the votes in favor of the accused, the other those against him."—*Id., IV, 3.*

The verdict against Jesus was also illegal because it was pronounced in the wrong place. Interpreting Deuteronomy 17: 8, 9 to mean that a sentence of death must be pronounced in a definite place chosen of God, the Jews selected for this purpose an apartment of the temple known as "The Hall of Gazith," or "the hall of hewn stone." Mendelsohn tells us that outside of this judgment hall no capital trial could be conducted, and no capital sentence pronounced. The law is: "A sentence of death can be pronounced only so long as the Sanhedrin holds its sessions in the appointed place."—*Maimonides, "Sanhedrin," XIV.* A sentence in the Talmud declares: "After leaving the hall Gazith no sentence of death can be passed upon anyone soever."—*Talmud, Bab., Abodah Zarah, or of Idolatry, chap. 1, fol. 8. (Chandler.)*

It is evident from the record that Jesus was tried and condemned in the palace of Caiaphas on Mount Zion, and not in the hall of hewn stone. Some modern Jewish writers, in order to defend the judges of Jesus, contend that His trial and condemnation must have been held in the proper place. Their only evidence is that the Hebrew law demanded it; therefore it must have been done. In refuting this contention, Edersheim, the Christian Jew, says: "There is truly not a tittle of evidence for the assumption of commentators, that Christ was led from the palace of Caiaphas into the council chamber. The whole proceedings took place in the former, and from it Christ was brought to Pilate."—*"The Life and Times of Jesus the Messiah," vol. 2, p. 556, note.*

Judges Guilty of Bribery

The Mosaic code was very severe on those who wrested judgment through bribery. Exodus 23: 1-8. In Hebrew law this was interpreted to include judges who gave bribes as well as received them. It has been the law of all nations in all ages that the giving or the receiving of bribes disqualifies a judge, and nullifies his verdict. The judges of Jesus had bribed Judas to deliver Him into their hands for a specified sum of money. Luke 22: 3-6. The amount agreed upon was "thirty pieces of silver," which was thirty of the silver shekels of the sanctuary, with a modern value of between $16 and $18 in United States money. Geikie declares that this was "the price of a slave." D. L. Moody once said that "God sent His only-begotten Son to ransom man; and man offered thirty pieces of silver for Him."

The evidence of the guilt of the judges of Jesus was demonstrated when Judas returned the bribe money and publicly confessed that he had "betrayed the innocent blood." Matthew 27: 1-6. In Acts 1: 19 we are told that this was done so publicly that "it was known unto all the dwellers at Jerusalem." The members of the Sanhedrin could not even deny their guilt. Judas had been a witness to the entire proceedings against Jesus, and the injustice of His treatment was so manifest and so flagrant that his conscience was smitten with guilt. He knew that Jesus was innocent, and the final sentence of death by acclamation was more than he could stand. He would now testify in behalf of Him who had had "no intercessor." "As the trial drew to a close, Judas could endure the torture of his guilty conscience no longer. Suddenly a hoarse voice rang through the hall, sending a thrill of terror to all hearts: He is innocent; spare Him, O Caiaphas! The tall form of Judas was now seen pressing through the startled throng. His face was pale and haggard, and great drops of sweat stood on his forehead. Rushing to the throne of judgment, he threw down before the high priest the pieces of silver that had been the price of his Lord's betrayal. . . . The perfidy of the priests was revealed. It was evident that they had bribed the disciple to betray his Master."—"*The Desire of Ages,*" *pages 721, 722.*

In his desperation Judas went out and hanged himself. What a tragic end to what could have been a useful and notable career! His name might have honored the pages of sacred history, and been emblazoned on the jeweled foundations of the Celestial City. Judas was covetous and selfish, and these sins proved his ruin. When he objected to the extravagance of Mary in anointing the feet of Jesus, the Scriptures declare of him: "The reason he said this was not that he cared for the poor, but that he was a thief, and that being in charge of the money box, he used to steal what was put into it." John 12: 6, Weymouth.

CHAPTER FOURTEEN

THE UNJUST SENTENCE

THE condemnation of Jesus by the Sanhedrin was illegal and unjust because the judges were disqualified to pass sentence upon Him. First of all, they were disqualified because of their enmity against the accused. Benny states the law of the Hebrews and of all nations when he says: "Nor under any circumstances, was a man known to be at enmity with the accused person permitted to occupy a position among his judges."—"*The Criminal Code of the Jews,*" *page 37.* This rule is further stated by Mendelsohn: "Nor must there be on the judicial bench either a relation, or a particular friend, or an *enemy* of either the accused or of the accuser." —"*The Criminal Jurisprudence of the Ancient Hebrews,*" *page 108. (Chandler.)*

This rule of law obtains among all peoples. If a defendant has the slightest reason to suspect the enmity of a judge, he can demand that his case be brought before another judge. In the language of I. M. Jost, the judges who tried and condemned Jesus were His "burning enemies." Within the six months previous to the trial, there had been at least three meetings of the Sanhedrin to plan His death. The first is recorded in John 7: 37-53. It was on this occasion that Nicodemus spoke in Christ's behalf and pleaded for justice. The second was only a few weeks before the trial, and is recorded in John 11: 41-53. The inspiration for this gathering was the resurrection of Lazarus, which had made a great stir among the people. The third council to plan the death of Christ was held just before the Passover, and is recorded in Luke 22: 1-3. The enmity of the judges was also proved by the bribing of Judas and the hiring of false witnesses. Jesus had been condemned, and even sentenced to die, before the trial ever began.

Christ's judges were also disqualified to pass judgment because most of them had been unfairly elected to office. Under Hebrew law the members of the Sanhedrin must be chosen because of their nobility of character. Their qualifications for office must measure up to a very strict code of rules. No selection to office in this august body was considered legal unless the candidate measured up to the qualifications specified by law. "The robe of the unfairly elected judge is to be respected not more than the blanket of the ass."—"*Hebrew Maxims and Rules,*" *Mendelsohn, page 182.* To safeguard the Sanhedrin from the elevation of mere politicians, who would make merchandise of their offices, Hebrew law provided no salary for any of its members. "As Moses sat in judgment without the expectation of material reward, so also must every judge act from a sense of duty only."—*Id., page 177.* (*Chandler.*)

It is a well-known fact that many of the judges of Jesus were not only degenerate and corrupt in character, but that they had purchased their seats in the council, and were making merchandise of their offices. In fact, several of them had grown rich by this means. This was especially true of the family of the high priest. "Now it is historically true that Annas and Caiaphas and their friends owned and controlled the stalls, booths, and bazaars connected with the temple and from which flowed a most lucrative trade. The profits from the sale of lambs and doves, sold for sacrifice, alone were enormous."—"*The Trial of Jesus,*" *Chandler, vol. 1, p. 304.* When Jesus denounced these men for making His Father's house "a house of merchandise" and "a den of thieves," and on two different occasions cleansed the temple of its unholy traffic, He not only wounded the pride and dignity of Annas and Caiaphas, but dealt a severe blow at their most lucrative source of income. This was one of the chief reasons for their bitter enmity.

Of the character of the members of the Sanhedrin that condemned Jesus, Rabbi Wise said: "The chief priests, under the iron rule of Pilate and his wicked master, Sejan, were the tools of the Roman soldiers who held Judea and Samaria in subjection. Like the high priest, they were appointed to and removed from office by the Roman governor of the country, either directly or indirectly. They purchased their commissions for high prices and, like almost all Roman appointees, used them for mercenary purposes. They were considered wicked men by the ancient writers, and must have stood very low in the estimation of the people over whom they tyrannized. The patriots must have looked upon them as hirelings of the foreign despot whose rule was abhorred. Although there was, here and there, a good, pious and patriotic man among them, he was an exception. As a general thing, and under the rule of Pilate, especially, they were the corrupt tools of a military despotism which Rome imposed upon enslaved Palestine."—"*The Martyrdom of Jesus*," *Wise*. (*Chandler*.)

Annas, a Sadducee

Speaking of Annas, Josephus declared him to be a Sadducee, "a sect particularly severe in its judgments." Of the responsibility of Annas and his sons in the death of Jesus, Renan wrote: "All his sons also were violent persecutors. One of them, named like his father, Hanan, caused James, the brother of the Lord, to be stoned, under circumstances not unlike those which surrounded the death of Jesus. The spirit of the family was haughty, bold, and cruel; it had that particular kind of proud and sullen wickedness which characterizes Jewish politicians."—"*Life of Jesus*," *page 326.* Annas' sons may have had part in condemning Jesus.

From the Talmud

The Talmud contains the following denunciation of the priestly families of the time of Christ: "What a plague is the family of Simon Boethus; cursed be their lances! What a plague is the family of Ananos; cursed be their hissing of vipers! What a plague is the family of Cantharus; cursed be their pens! What a plague is the family of Ismael ben Phabi; cursed be their fists! They are high priests themselves, their sons are treasurers, their sons-in-law are commanders, and their servants strike the people with staves." "The porch of the sanctuary cried out four times. The first time, Depart from here, descendants of Eli; ye pollute the temple of the Eternal! The second time, Let Issachar ben Keifar Barchi depart from here, who polluted himself and profaneth the victims consecrated to God! The third time, Widen yourselves, ye gates of the sanctuary, and let Israel ben Phabi, the willful enter, that he may discharge the functions of the priesthood! Yet another cry was heard, Widen yourselves, ye gates, and let Ananias ben Nebedeus the gourmand enter, that he may glut himself on the victims!"—"*Pesachim*," *or* "*of the Passover*," *fol. 57, verso.* (*Chandler.*) See also "Jesus Before the Sanhedrin," Lemann, pages 54, 55; "The Life and Words of Christ," Geikie, pages 240, 241, 736-738; "The Trial of Jesus," Chandler, vol. 1, pp. 297, 298. Some of these men, and others like them, were among the judges who tried and condemned Jesus. Is it any wonder that He said in prophecy: "The floods of ungodly men made Me afraid"? Psalm 18: 4.

Hebrew law demanded not only that every consideration possible be given to the merits of the defense, but also that every effort be made to find evidence in behalf of the defendant. This rule is based on Deuteronomy 13: 14. In the Mishna we are told that "the judges shall weigh the matter in the sincerity of their conscience."—"*Sanhedrin,*" *IV, 5.* All the efforts of the judges must be in behalf of the accused, who was condemned only when the evidence against him was conclusive and overwhelming so that there was no other course possible. "The primary object of the Hebrew judicial system was to render the conviction of an innocent person impossible. All the ingenuity of the Jewish legists was directed to the attainment of this end."—"*The Criminal Code of the Jews,*" *Benny, page 56.* (*Chandler.*) Jesus was condemned to die because He claimed to be the Messiah. Since all the judges of Jesus were expecting their Messiah at that very time, it was their duty to examine His claim in the light of the Scriptures and His works.

The People in Expectation

In Luke 3: 15 we are told that when John the Baptist proclaimed his message, "the people were in expectation, and all men mused in their hearts of John, whether he were the Christ, or not." One of the chief prophecies on which this hope was based was Genesis 49: 10. "The dying words of Jacob filled them with hope: 'The scepter shall not depart from Judah, nor a lawgiver from between his feet, until Shiloh come.' The waning power of Israel testified that the Messiah's coming was at hand. . . . While few understood the nature of Christ's mission, there was a widespread expectation of a mighty prince who should establish his kingdom in Israel, and who should come as a deliverer to the nations."—"*The Desire of Ages,*" *page 34.*

WATCHING FOR THE MESSIAH'S ADVENT

Based on Jacob's dying prophecy, the Jews had long been watching for two great signs that would proclaim the Messiah's advent at hand. The first of these was the departure of the scepter from Judah, or the loss of the kingly crown and authority by the kingdom of Judah. This sign was fulfilled when the crown was removed from the head of the last king of Judah by Nebuchadnezzar, king of Babylon. Ezekiel 21:26, 27. This sign had been fulfilled more than five hundred years before the birth of Christ. The Talmud declared that "the Son of David shall not come unless the royal power has been taken away from Judah."—"*Sanhedrin,*" *fol. 97, verso.* For more than half a millennium the Jews had been watching for the second sign.

The second sign would be the loss of judicial authority, or the power to make and enforce laws. Said the Talmud: "The Son of David shall not come unless the judges have ceased in Israel."—*Ibid.* (*Chandler.*) This sign was fulfilled in 6 A. D., when Judea became a Roman province under the rulership of a Roman governor, or procurator. At this date King Archelaus was deposed, and the Sanhedrin was stripped of its judicial authority, the power of life and death being also taken from it. The Sanhedrin was no longer the "lawgiver" of the nation. That office had now passed to Rome. Both signs had therefore been fulfilled, and at the time of the trial of Jesus all the Jews were expecting the appearance of their Messiah.

Not only had the kingly scepter passed from Judah and

the lawgiver from between his feet, as Jesus stood before the Sanhedrin claiming to be the promised and looked-for Messiah, but there were many other evidences that His judges should have examined before passing sentence. Jesus was born in Bethlehem in fulfillment of prophecy. Micah 5: 2; Matthew 2: 1; Luke 2: 4-7. Prophecy also declared that He would be born of a virgin. Isaiah 7: 14; Matthew 1: 24, 25. He was also born of the house of David. Jeremiah 23: 5, 6; Matthew 1: 20. His advent was heralded by a forerunner like Elijah. Malachi 3: 1; Isaiah 40: 3; Matthew 3: 1-3; Luke 7: 27, 28. In harmony with the prediction of the Messiah, Jesus began His preaching in Galilee. Isaiah 9: 1, 2; Matthew 4: 12-17. His mighty miracles also declared Him to be the Messiah. Isaiah 35: 5, 6; Matthew 12: 22; Luke 5: 24, 25. The public entry of Jesus into Jerusalem had been foretold. Zechariah 9: 9; Matthew 21: 6-9. His betrayal by one of His disciples for thirty pieces of silver was another sign. Psalm 41: 9; Zechariah 11: 12, 13; Matthew 26: 14, 15; 27: 3-8. The Messiah was also to be a man of sorrow, poverty, and suffering. Isaiah 53: 3; Mark 15: 19, 20; Luke 9: 58. Besides these, the visit of the Wise Men, the attempt to destroy Him at birth, the flight into Egypt, and, in fact, almost every event of the life of Jesus was a fulfillment of prophecies identifying Him as the expected Messiah. Many of these facts were known to the judges, and all of them could have been known by investigation and proved by witnesses. But not a witness was called to defend Jesus or to testify regarding His claims.

The gross injustice of the entire proceedings against Jesus before the supreme court of the Jews is graphically summed up by two noted lawyers. "Dupin, in his tract on the 'Trial of Jesus Before the Sanhedrin,' . . . has satisfactorily shown that throughout the whole course of that trial the rules of the Jewish law of procedure were grossly violated, and that the accused was deprived of rights, belonging even to the meanest citizen. He was arrested in the night, bound as a malefactor, beaten before His arraignment, and struck in open court during the trial; He was tried on a feast day, and before sunrise; He was compelled to criminate Himself, and this, under an oath of solemn judicial adjuration; and He was sentenced on the same day of the conviction. In all these particulars the law was wholly disregarded."—"*The Testimony of the Evangelists,*" *Greenleaf, page 566.*

Rosadi says of the injustice of the Hebrew trial: "Grasping priests denounced Him, false witnesses accused Him, judges of bad faith condemned Him; a friend betrayed Him; no one defended Him; He was dragged with every kind of contumely and violence to the malefactor's cross, where He spoke the last words of truth and brotherhood among men. It was one of the greatest and most memorable acts of injustice."—"*The Trial of Jesus,*" *page 1.*

With the unanimous sentence of death by the Hebrew judges there came to a close the greatest travesty on justice in the history of mankind. The condemnation of Jesus constituted the final act of the Jewish nation in the rejection of their own Messiah. He had come "unto His own, and His own received Him not." He was "despised and rejected of men." The Jews could not execute their own sentence of death, so they turned Jesus over to the Roman authorities, charging Him with blasphemy against the God of the Hebrews and high treason against the emperor of Rome. Before the Roman tribunal took place the second phase of the judicial mockery staining the records of two great legal systems.

CHAPTER FIFTEEN

JESUS BEFORE PILATE

THE power to execute capital sentence had been taken from the Sanhedrin by the Roman authorities. For this reason the sentence of death pronounced upon Jesus by the Jews had to be confirmed and executed by the Roman governor. As soon as the Hebrew judges had declared Jesus to be worthy of death, "they led Him away, and delivered Him to Pontius Pilate the governor." "And Jesus stood before the governor." Matthew 27: 2, 11. In his record of this event, John says, "It was early." John 18: 28, 29. It was still in the fourth watch, which lasted from three to six o'clock. It was probably between five and six o'clock the morning of Nisan 14, Hebrew time, when the rabble, under the leadership of the chief dignitaries of the Jews, led Jesus to the palace of Pilate, the Roman governor of the province of Judea, where the final act in the awful drama of judicial injustice was to be enacted. Hebrew law did not permit the execution of a death sentence the same day it was pronounced; but, if the Roman authorities did the executing, the Jews doubtless felt that they were relieved of the responsibility.

The capital of the province of Judea was at Cæsarea, which was therefore the official residence of the governor. He spent but a few days each year in Jerusalem, usually during the great national festivals of the Jews when the danger of insurrection was the greatest. The Jews at this time were a very turbulent people, who were embittered because of the loss of their kingly and judicial authority, and were seething with discontent under the galling yoke of a foreign despotism. During the national festivals, when vast multitudes assembled from all parts of Judea and from other lands, the national aspirations of the Jews were always rekindled. Josephus estimated the number attending a single Passover at 2,700,000, including the population of Jerusalem. The governor deemed it wise to be present on these occasions with additional cohorts of Roman soldiers to meet any sudden emergency.

Descriptions of Palace

During these visits to Jerusalem, Pilate occupied the palace of Herod on Mount Zion, for, according to Josephus, it was the official residence of the procurators of the province while they were in the city. Another writer says: "They lodged in the palace of Herod, which, henceforth, was called the prætorium, and became the residence of the procurators when they were in Jerusalem at the time of the feasts, for, except then, they lived in Cæsarea."—"*The Life and Words of Christ,*" *Geikie, page 194.* This palace was built by Herod the Great, one of the greatest builders of his time. It was located in the northwest quarter of the city, on the heights of Zion whence could be had a beautiful panoramic view of the city and surrounding country. The palace was also known as the king's castle and the prætorium. Theodor Keim describes it as "a tyrant's stronghold and in part a fairy pleasure house." Being the most magnificent residence in the city, it was the pride of Jerusalem.

Geikie declares that the palace of Herod was located "about the center of the northern half of Mount Zion, a great part of which was enclosed within its park walls, themselves a second line of defense, forty-five feet in height, with strong towers rising, at equal distances, from their broad tops. The palace itself was indescribably magnificent. Spacious rooms, with elaborately carved walls and ceilings, many of them crusted with precious stones, displayed Oriental splendor to hundreds of guests at a time. Gold and silver shone on every side. Round this sumptuous abode porticoes with curious pillars of costly stone offered shady retreats. Groves and gardens stretched on every side, intermingled with pools and artificial rivers, bordered by long, delightful walks, frequented, through the day, by all who could endure the desecration of Jerusalem by the countless statues which adorned them."—"*The Life and Words of Christ*," *page 146*.

Josephus' Description

Of this beautiful palace Josephus wrote: " 'The kinds of stone used in its construction were countless. Whatever was rare abounded in it. The roofs astonished everyone by the length of their beams, and the beauty of their adornment. Vessels, mostly of gold and silver, rich in chasing, shone on every side. The great dining hall had been constructed to supply table couches for three hundred guests. Others opened in all directions, each with a different style of pillar. The open space before the palace was laid out in broad walks, planted with long avenues of different trees, and bordered by broad, deep canals and great ponds, flowing with cool, clear water, and set off along the banks with innumerable works of art.' "—*Quoted in* "*The Life and Words of Christ*," *Geikie, page 735*. It was to the gate of this magnificent palace that Jesus was brought to have the Sanhedrin's sentence of death confirmed and ordered executed by the governor.

Palestine was conquered by Pompey in 63 B. C., and

placed under the dominion of Rome. In the year 6 A. D. Judea was made a Roman province under the rulership of procurators, or governors, of whom Pilate was the sixth. The procurators were appointed by the emperor, and were sent out from Rome as his personal representatives. No province of the empire was more difficult to rule than Judea, and it needed a man who was vigilant and tactful, and with an iron will. The very belief of the Jews that their kingdom and throne would stand forever, and that the Messiah would soon appear to break the Roman yoke and rule the world, made Judea the hotbed of sedition and the birthplace of pretenders to kingly power. Several insurrections had already taken place, and more were momentarily expected.

By birth Pilate was a Spaniard, having come from Seville, one of the cities of Spain enjoying the right of Roman citizenship. Like Saul of Tarsus, Pilate was "born free" because he was born in a "free city." His father's name was Marcus Pontius. He had distinguished himself as a general under Agrippa by leading a troop of renegades against their former comrades. As a reward he was given the pilum (javelin), a Roman decoration of honor for heroic military service. To commemorate this medal of valor, the family took the name of Pilati, or Pilatus, or Pilate. The son, Lucius Pontius Pilate, distinguished himself as a soldier in the German campaigns of Germanicus. At the conclusion of the war, young Pilate went to Rome more fully to satisfy his ambitions for adventure and romance, and, if possible, to secure a political office with its rewards of honor and fortune.

Pilate, the "Javelinman," had not been long in the metropolis of the world when he became acquainted with Claudia, the youngest daughter of Julia, the daughter of Augustus Cæsar. After being married to Tiberius, her third husband, Julia was banished from Rome and sent into exile by her own father, the emperor, because of her wicked and dissolute life. She was one of the lewdest and coarsest women in Rome, and, according to Suetonius, nothing so embittered the life of Augustus as did the shameful conduct of his own daughter. Whenever she was mentioned to Augustus during her exile he would say, "Would I were wifeless, or had childless died." While Julia was in exile, Claudia was born, illegitimate, her father being a Roman knight. When she was about thirteen years of age, her mother sent her to Rome to be reared in the court of Tiberius, who, through pretense and intrigue, had become emperor on the death of Augustus. Claudia was about sixteen when Pontius Pilate arrived in Rome. Whether Pilate was attracted to Claudia because of his love for her, or for the purpose of advancing his own selfish interests, we do not know. But considering his greedy and selfish character in the light of his later conduct, we have a strong suspicion of an ulterior motive. His marriage into the royal family was doubtless a means to an end, which was that of securing an appointment to political office.

Pilate's marriage into the royal family won for him the office of procurator of Judea. According to the story, when the bridal party came out of the temple where the ceremony was celebrated and Lucius Pontius started to follow his bride into the imperial litter, Tiberius, who was one of the twelve witnesses required to attend the ceremony, held him back and handed him a document which he had taken from his bosom. It was the wedding present,—the governorship of Judea,—with orders to proceed at once to Cæsarea to take over the office made vacant by the recall of Valerius Gratus. This was in the year 26 A. D. Pilate was notified that his ship was waiting to take him to his province, and he had to leave without again seeing his bride until she joined him later at Cæsarea. It was by special permission of Tiberius that Claudia was allowed to join her husband; for, by imperial decree, the wives of governors had not been permitted to accompany them to the provinces. This restriction was later withdrawn because it gradually fell into disuse. The attempt of the Senate to re-enact the regulation ended in failure.

Pilate was untrained in political office, and he began his reign with a series of blunders that brought upon him the intense hatred of the Jews. Regarding these mistakes The Cambridge Bible, commenting on Luke 23: 1, says: "His very first act—the bringing of the silver eagles and other insignia of the Legions from Cæsarea to Jerusalem—a step which he was obliged to retract—had caused fierce exasperation between him and the Jews. This had been increased by his application of money from the corban, or sacred treasury, to the secular purpose of bringing water to Jerusalem from the Pools of Solomon (see xiii. 4). In consequence of this quarrel Pilate sent his soldiers among the mob with concealed daggers (a fatal precedent for the Sicarii), and there had been a great massacre. A third tumult had been caused by his placing gilt votive shields dedicated to the emperor Tiberius, in his residence at Jerusalem. The Jews regarded these as idolatrous, and he had been obliged by the emperor's orders to remove them. He had also had deadly quarrels with the Samaritans, whom he had attacked on Mount Gerizim in a movement stirred up by a Messianic impostor; and with the Galileans 'whose blood he had mingled with their sacrifices' (xiii. 1). He reflected the hatred felt toward the Jews by his patron Sejanus, and had earned the character which Philo gives him of being a savage, inflexible, and arbitrary ruler."

The predecessors of Pilate had exercised great care to avoid offense to the Jews because of their religious ideas. The proud and tactless Pilate defied the sacred sentiments of those he had come to govern. To his chagrin and dishonor, he was compelled to retract and correct his mistakes because of the threatening attitude of the populace, and on the order of Tiberius, to whom the Jews had appealed. These experiences served only to increase Pilate's hatred for the Jews, and theirs for him. Both Josephus and Philo have left on record a very ugly picture of the character of Pilate. Philo Judæus, a Jewish philosopher who was a contemporary of Pilate, charges him with "corruptibility, violence, robberies, ill-treatment of the people, grievances, continuous executions without even the form of a trial, endless and intolerable cruelties." He further declared Pilate to be a man of "stubborn and harsh quality" who "could not bring himself to do anything that might cause pleasure to the Jews."—"*De Legatione ad Cajum,*" *ed. Hoesch, page 1034.* Dr. Charles J. Ellicott says that Pilate was "self-seeking and cowardly; able to perceive what was right, but without moral strength to follow it out."—"*Historical Lectures on the Life of Our Lord Jesus Christ,*" *6th ed., page 350.*

Geikie declared that Pilate was "venal, covetous, cruel, even to delighting in blood, without principle or remorse, and yet wanting decision at critical moments."—"*The Life and Words of Christ,*" *page 205.* Rosadi said of the character of the Roman governor who sent Jesus to the cross: "Lucius Pontius was the son of a renegade soldier; he himself was a renegade husband. He inherited the servility of his father, who had great ambitions at the court of Rome. He was personally tainted by the most shady court intrigues. . . . Every act of his official life is inspired by the necessary program of adaptation, and not by the spontaneous leanings of his own nature. His character, it is true, was reft of every moral sense, if we may judge it by its deeds, and was prepared for any degree of base dissimulation."—*"The Trial of Jesus," page 217.*

Another writer describes Pilate as a typical politician: "If now we wish to form a judgment of Pilate's character, we easily see that he was one of that large class of men who aspire to public offices, not from a pure and lofty desire of benefiting the public and advancing the good of the world, but from selfish and personal considerations, from a love of distinction, from a love of power, from a love of self-indulgence; being destitute of any fixed principles, and having no aim but office and influence, they act right only by chance, and when convenient, and are wholly incapable of pursuing a consistent course, or of acting with firmness and self-denial in cases in which the preservation of integrity requires the exercise of these qualities. Pilate was obviously a man of weak, and therefore, with his temptations, of corrupt character."—*The Popular and Critical Bible Encyclopedia and Scriptural Dictionary, vol. 3, edited by the Right Reverend Samuel Fallows, A. M., D. D., LL. D., art. "Pilate."*

Chandler uses the character and experience of Pilate as a warning to the youth of this generation: "And now, in the supreme moment of his life and of history, from his nerveless grasp fell the reigns of fate and fortune that destiny had placed within his hands. Called upon to play a leading role in the mighty drama of the universe, his craven cowardice made him a pitiable and contemptible figure. A splendid example this, the conduct of Pilate, for the youth of the world, not to imitate but to shun! Let the young men of America and of all the earth remember that a crisis is allotted to every life. It may be a great one or a small one, but it will come either invited or unbidden. . . . Let the young aspirant for the glories of the earth and the rewards of heaven remember that youth is the time for the formation of that courage and the gathering of that strength of which victory is born. Let him remember that if he degrades his physical and spiritual manhood in early life, the coming of the great day of his existence will make him another Pilate—cringing, crouching, and contemptible."—"*The Trial of Jesus*," *vol. 2, pp. 90, 91.*

This was the judge to whom the Jews delivered Jesus in order that their sentence of death might be ratified and executed. After ruthlessly disregarding every principle of Hebrew law in their own trial, they handed Jesus over to a judge whom they detested but whose reputation for cruelty and injustice gave them confidence that he would do their bidding even if it required the pressure of a threatened appeal to Tiberius.

CHAPTER SIXTEEN

ROMAN LAW IN CHRIST'S DAY

As we shall soon consider the trial of Jesus before the tribunal of Rome, it will be profitable to discuss briefly the principles of Roman law. The knowledge of what should have been done during the trial places a greater emphasis upon the illegalities of the proceedings and the injustice of the decision.

A procurator was permitted to use either Roman or local law in administering the affairs of the province, except in cases of treason, when only Roman law could be applied. As far as possible, the governors of provinces employed the laws with which the people were already familiar. But Jesus was charged by the Jews with the crime of treason against the Roman government, and therefore He had to be tried according to the rules of Roman law.

Jesus had been condemned as guilty of death by the Hebrew tribunal on the charge of blasphemy. This was the only indictment on which the Jews had been able to agree on a verdict. But a religious charge would have no weight in a Roman court; so once more the indictment is changed to suit the occasion and accomplish the purpose of the enemies of the Christ. He now stands at the judgment bar of Rome charged with the crime of high treason against Cæsar. "And now upon His life before He descended into the tomb, Rome, the mother of laws, and Jerusalem, the destroyer of prophets, sat in judgment."—*"The Trial of Jesus," Chandler, vol. 2, p. 3.* In regard to Roman law and jurisprudence the same writer said: "The Roman judicial system is incomparable in the history of jurisprudence. Judea gave religion, Greece gave letters, and Rome gave laws to mankind. Thus runs the judgment of the world."—*Id., page 5.*

Fortunately we know how a Roman trial of a capital case was conducted in the city of Rome, and the same procedure was supposed to be followed in the provinces. The court in the capital of the empire was the model for the entire Roman world. The procurators were appointed to office by the emperor, and according to his will they could be relieved of their responsibilities. As his personal representatives, the procurators administered the law in his stead. "It is also certain that in the provinces the same order was observed in criminal cases as was observed in cases tried at Rome."—"*The Trial of Jesus,*" *Rosadi, page 293.*

The Question of Procedure

No people had a finer sense of justice than did the Romans, and they prided themselves on their strict adherence to the rules of law without fear or favor. Since from many reliable sources we know the procedure of a Roman trial in the case of treason, there can be no question as to the duty of Pilate during the trial of Jesus. Dr. Gustave Geib declares that "a description of the proceedings in the permanent tribunals is . . . to be regarded as a description of the proceedings in the provincial courts." In his book, "The Legal Procedure of Cicero's Time," page 413, Greenidge says: "The criminal procedure of the provinces was . . . closely modeled on that of Rome." (Chandler.) It must be presumed that Pilate knew the proper procedure of a trial for treason; therefore, his violations of the rules of Roman law were willful and malicious.

The following are the nine successive steps usually taken

in the trial of criminal cases in the permanent courts of Rome.

1. The application to the presiding magistrate or praetor for permission to bring criminal charges against a certain person. Under Roman law there were no regular prosecutors. Private citizens preferred the charges and prosecuted the case.

2. If there was more than one accuser, a preliminary hearing was held to determine which one should prosecute the case.

3. A private preliminary hearing was held in order that the president of the court might obtain a more complete and definite knowledge of the charges.

4. The framing of the indictment or inscription by the prosecutor and his witnesses.

5. The formal presentation of the indictment to the presiding judge and the fixing of the time for the trial.

6. The beginning of the proceedings on the day appointed for the trial. The judges or jurors were summoned by heralds.

7. The impaneling of the jury or judges, which was done by placing the names of a number of citizens on tablets, depositing them in an urn, and then drawing out the number required.

8. The proceedings of the trial, which was conducted in the Forum, where seats were placed for the judges. Roman cases could be conducted only during the day, from daybreak to an hour before sunset.

9. The decision of the judges who voted by ballot, using black and white stones, the white for acquittal and the black for condemnation.

While all these rules could not be applied in every case in the provinces, the provincial judges were supposed to follow them to the best of their ability. The principles of justice and equity that formed the foundations of Roman law were intended to make injustice impossible in any part of the Roman Empire. But, as in modern times, the great question was not in regard to the law, but rather to the administering of the law, which depended wholly on the character of the judges. Judges who love justice will seldom find any law a barrier to right decisions.

The Right of Appeal

Under the rule of the Cæsars only Roman citizens had the right to appeal certain cases from the decision of the procurator to the emperor. Paul was able to exercise this power because he was a Roman citizen. When he said to Governor Festus, "I stand at Cæsar's judgment seat, where I ought to be judged. . . . I appeal unto Cæsar," the procurator of Judea was obliged to comply with the request and send Paul to Rome to go on trial before Nero. Later, when the case was reviewed before King Agrippa, Festus said: "When I found that he had committed nothing worthy of death, and that he himself hath appealed to Augustus, I have determined to send him." Acts 25: 10, 11, 25.

But Jesus was not a Roman citizen; therefore the decision of Pilate in His case was final. The power of appeal is one of the greatest safeguards to justice in every land, as it exercises a constant restraining influence over the judges. Procurators always dreaded to have cases appealed to the emperor, as it cast a reflection on their ability to rule and to judge. This was especially true when their decisions were reversed by the supreme judge of the Romans. The same restraining influence safeguards justice in the decisions of modern judges. A judge is justly proud of his record when none of his decisions have been reversed by a higher court. The right of appeal accounts for the difference in the treatment of Paul before Felix and Festus and that accorded Jesus in His trial before Pilate. The power of appeal was not hanging threateningly over the head of the one who was to judge Jesus.

Roman law provided several forms of capital punishment, the principal ones being beheading, burning, drowning, and crucifixion. The penalty for treason, the worst of all crimes under Roman law, was crucifixion—the most frightful of all punishments. Geikie says of this mode of death: "Death by the cross was the most terrible and the most dreaded and shameful punishment of antiquity—a punishment, the very name of which, Cicero tells us, should never come near the thoughts, the eyes, or ears, of a Roman citizen, far less his person. It was of Eastern origin, and had been in use among the Persians and Carthaginians, long before its employment in Western countries. Alexander the Great adopted it in Palestine, from the Phœnicians, after the defense of Tyre, which he punished by crucifying two thousand citizens, when the place surrendered. Crassus signalized its introduction into Roman use by lining the road from Capua to Rome with crucified slaves, captured in the revolt of Spartacus, and Augustus finally inaugurated its general use, by crucifying six thousand slaves at once, in Sicily, in his suppression of the war raised by Sextus Pompeius."—*"The Life and Words of Christ," pages 775, 776.*

Of the use of the cross as an instrument of punishment among the ancients, and its meaning to Christians, Chandler wrote: "Crucifixion. Around this word gather the most frightful memories and, at the same time, the sweetest and sublimest hopes of the human race. A thorough appreciation of the trial of Jesus, it is felt, renders necessary an exhaustive treatment of the punishment in which all the horrors and illegalities of the proceedings against Him culminated.

"*History.*—Tradition attributes the origin of crucifixion, the most frightful and inhuman form of punishment ever known, to a woman, Semiramis, queen of Assyria. . . . Crucifixion was practiced by the ancient Egyptians, Carthaginians, Persians, Germans, Assyrians, Greeks, and Romans. The Romans employed this form of punishment on a colossal scale. The Roman general Varus crucified 2,000 Jews in one day at the gates of Jerusalem. The close of the war with Spartacus, the gladiator, witnessed the crucifixion of 10,000 slaves between Capua and Rome. . . . Only the vilest criminals, among free men, such as were guilty of robbery, piracy, assassination, perjury, sedition, treason, and desertion from the army, met death in this way. The *jus civitatis* protected Roman citizens against this punishment."—"*The Trial of Jesus,*" *vol. 2, pp. 54, 55.*

In describing his love for Christ, the apostle Paul said that he longed to know "the fellowship of His sufferings" and be "made conformable unto His death." Philippians 3:10. "I long to know Christ and the power which is in His resurrection, and to share in His sufferings and die even as He died," is the Weymouth translation. But because Paul was a Roman citizen, the privilege of being crucified and thus suffering the same death as his Master was denied him. He was beheaded, which was a punishment meted out to Roman citizens. Tradition tells us that when Peter was about to be crucified, he declared that because of his denial of Jesus he was not worthy to suffer the same death, and at his request he was crucified head downward. The love of the early Christians for their divine Lord should put most modern believers to shame.

CHAPTER SEVENTEEN

JESUS ACQUITTED BY PILATE

"THEN led they Jesus from Caiaphas unto the hall of judgment: and it was early; and they themselves went not into the judgment hall, lest they should be defiled; but that they might eat the Passover. Pilate then went out unto them, and said, What accusation bring ye against this Man?" John 18: 28, 29.

One of the wings of the palace of Herod contained an assembly room known as the judgment hall or the "praetorium." It was about sunrise when the Jewish rabble arrived at the gate of the palace of Herod, to ask the governor to confirm their sentence of death against Jesus, and to order its execution. At the door of the praetorium the Jews halted, for the Passover preparation had already begun, and they dared not enter a Gentile building for fear of being polluted. Their own trial in the palace of Caiaphas had been marked by more than a score of judicial blunders, when the most fundamental principles of Hebrew law had been ruthlessly trampled underfoot; and yet they scrupled to violate a mere ritual regulation concerning ceremonial defilement! Such contradictory conduct gives force to the saying, "Consistency, thou art a jewel." We must not forget that the Roman trial of Jesus took place outside the gate, and not in the praetorium.

Pilate asked: "What accusation bring ye against this Man? They answered and said unto him, If He were not a malefactor, we would not have delivered Him up unto thee. Then said Pilate unto them, Take ye Him, and judge Him according to your law. The Jews therefore said unto him,

It is not lawful for us to put any man to death." John 18:29-31.

Pilate had often sentenced men to death "without the semblance of a trial," and had doubtless more than once confirmed the decisions of the Sanhedrin without even an investigation. The Jews had hoped that on this occasion he would give orders for the crucifixion of Jesus without asking any questions. To influence him to make such a decision, the chief dignitaries of the Jews attended the prisoner.

To the surprise and consternation of the Jews, Pilate demanded the charges against Jesus. He took them by surprise by asking for a formal indictment. They attempted to evade the question of the judge, and intimated that their trial and sentence were sufficient evidence of His guilt; if He had not been a criminal, they would never have brought Him to receive sentence. To this insolent reply the governor, with withering sarcasm, told the Jews that if their judgment and sentence were enough, they had better do the executing also. He virtually told them that if they refused to prefer specific charges, he would not deal with the case. The acknowledgement of their loss of authority to impose and to execute capital sentence was music in Pilate's ears. His demand had drawn from the Jews the admission that they were more interested in the death of Jesus Christ than in His having a fair trial before the judicial bodies.

Jesus and Pilate had never met before, but they were not unknown to each other. Through his officers and soldiers, Pilate had been kept informed regarding the movements, miracles, and teachings of Jesus during the previous three and a half years. Some of Pilate's centurions or members of their families had been healed by Jesus, and the reports they brought to Pilate had given him a very favorable impression of the popular Teacher, whom many hoped and believed was the Messiah. The governor had also been informed of Christ's scathing rebukes and unsparing denunciations of the scribes and rulers of the Jews, and he fully approved. He felt that he and Jesus had some feelings in common. When the searching eyes of Pilate met those of the prisoner, his keen perception immediately told him that before him stood the innocent victim of a cruel conspiracy. He had never before beheld such a noble countenance, and he was determined carefully to investigate the case before passing sentence. Jesus, of course, was well acquainted with the character and deeds of the procurator, and with his cruel and unjust rule. He also knew how bitterly the Jews hated him, and he the Jews.

The Charges

"The whole multitude of them arose, and led Him unto Pilate. And they began to accuse Him, saying, We found this fellow perverting the nation, and forbidding to give tribute to Cæsar, saying that He Himself is Christ a King." Luke 23: 1, 2. The confusion and embarrassment occasioned by Pilate's demand for the indictment soon passed away. The accusers of Jesus knew that a religious charge would have no weight with the governor, as was later demonstrated when the Jews brought Paul before Gallio, the governor of Achaia, and charged him with persuading men "to worship God contrary to the law." Acts 18: 12-16. Pilate, too, would have refused to be a judge "of such matters." The Jews had condemned Jesus on the charge of blasphemy; but, to meet the emergency of a change of jurisdiction, they suddenly changed their accusation from a religious to a political offense. Three charges were made, and all of them were forms of treason against the Roman government and ruler.

The first charge in the indictment was a revival of the sedition or insurrection accusation, which they had so signally failed to substantiate in their own court. "We found this fellow perverting the nation" was an intimation that they had caught Him in the act. The second count in the indictment was even more serious and treasonable because to refuse to pay taxes, and especially to teach others thus to deny the authority of the ruling government, was equivalent to a defiance of the laws and sovereignty of Rome. Both Ulpian and Cicero declared that such conduct was treason. The charge, of course, was untrue. The Jews had attempted to get Jesus to do the very thing they were now charging Him with, and had failed. Luke 20: 19-26. The third charge was the most serious of all, for any unauthorized claim of kingship was high treason against Cæsar. This was the gravest offense known to Roman law, and was deserving of the severest punishment.

As the personal representative of Tiberius Cæsar in the Judean province, Pilate could not ignore these charges of treason against his suspicious master. Chandler writes that Tiberius Cæsar was "a morbid and capricious tyrant, whose fretful and suspicious temper would kindle into fire at the slightest suggestion of treason in any quarter. Tacitus records fifty-two cases of prosecution for treason during his reign. . . . The most harmless acts were at times construed into an affront to the majesty or into an assault upon the safety of this miserable despot."—*"The Trial of Jesus," vol. 2, p. 70.* Such charges were especially serious because of the political situation existing at that time in Judea. "During the life of Jesus, Judea was passing through a period of great religious and political excitement. The Messiah was expected and a king was hoped for; and numerous pretenders appeared from time to time. The Roman governors were constantly on the outlook for acts of sedition and treason." —*Id., page 110.*

The Case Examined

"Then Pilate entered into the judgment hall again, and called Jesus, and said unto Him, Art Thou the King of the Jews? Jesus answered him, Sayest thou this thing of thyself, or did others tell it thee of Me? Pilate answered, Am I a Jew? Thine own nation and the chief priests have delivered Thee unto me: what hast Thou done? Jesus answered, My kingdom is not of this world: if My kingdom were of this world, then would My servants fight, that I should not be delivered to the Jews: but now is My kingdom not from hence. Pilate therefore said unto Him, Art Thou a king then? Jesus answered, Thou sayest that I am a king. To this end was I born, and for this cause came I into the world, that I should bear witness unto the truth. Every one that is of the truth heareth My voice. Pilate saith unto Him, What is truth? And when he had said this, he went out again unto the Jews, and saith unto them, I find in Him no fault at all." John 18: 33-38.

As soon as Pilate had heard the charges, especially the one regarding Christ's claim to kingship, he led the prisoner back into the judgment hall where he could conduct an examination unmolested by the noisy rabble. In answer to his first question as to whether Jesus claimed to be the King of the Jews, Jesus wanted to know if the question was asked from the viewpoint of the Romans or of the Jews. If Pilate had in mind, in asking the question, a temporal kingdom that would be a rival of Rome, then the answer would be in the negative. If, on the other hand, the kingdom referred to was spiritual, the answer would be in the affirmative. Dupin declared that "in reality, Jesus was desirous of knowing, first of all, the authors of this new accusation—Is this an accusation brought against Me by the *Romans* or by the *Jews?*" (Greenleaf.)

Three times in the interview Jesus acknowledged that He was a king, and three times He told Pilate that His kingdom was not of this world. In this He assured the governor that He was not a rival for the throne of Cæsar, and that His kingdom would not by force supplant the rule of Rome. Jesus assured Pilate that he had no reason to fear sedition or a political revolt because of any ambitions He had for political office. He was the King of truth, and His leadership had to do only with spiritual affairs. As evidence of these things, Jesus reminded Pilate of the fact that He had no army. If He had kingly ambitions, He would by this time have had a military force to compel recognition of His claims. Pilate may have known that Jesus had refused the offer of kingship by the great multitude when He had miraculously fed them, and that He had also rebuked the disciple who attempted to defend Him, compelling him to put up his sword.

The Acquittal

As the result of the private interview, Pilate was thoroughly convinced that Jesus was not only innocent of the charges made against Him, but that He was the victim of a plot to do away with Him by any means possible. He knew that the conspiracy had been inspired by hatred and jealousy. He therefore did not wait for an answer to his last question, but went back to the entrance of the praetorium, and handed down a decision of acquittal in the words, "I find in Him no fault at all." It may be that the clamoring of the mob at the gateway cut short the interview. It would be interesting to know what Christ's answer would have been to the question, "What is truth?" But Pilate may have asked the question in sarcasm.

Regarding the decision of Pilate, the noted legal authority, Greenleaf, said: "Here was a sentence of acquittal, judicially pronounced, and irreversible, except by a higher power, upon appeal; and it was the duty of Pilate thereupon to have discharged Him."—"*The Testimony of the Evangelists*," *page 565.* It was clearly the duty of the governor to enforce his decision, and to protect Jesus from the fury of the mob. One word and a detachment of Roman soldiers would have dispersed the Jews, and established the authority of the judge. But Pilate did not do his duty when the Jews did not accept his decision. The failure to enforce his decree was the first of a series of judicial irregularities that gave Pilate his place in history as "the unjust judge."

CHAPTER EIGHTEEN

CHRIST BEFORE KING HEROD

As soon as Pilate had handed down the decision of acquittal in the trial of Jesus, the Jews were furious. They not only refused to accept the verdict, but they preferred new charges. "Then said Pilate to the chief priests and to the people, I find no fault in this Man. And they were the more fierce, saying, He stirreth up the people, teaching throughout all Jewry, beginning from Galilee to this place." Luke 23:4, 5. Pilate should have given no attention to further charges after having dismissed the case. "No man shall be put twice in jeopardy," is a judicial maxim that has come down to us from the Romans. The new charges were doubtless agreed upon by the Jews while Jesus and Pilate were in the judgment hall, and for just such an emergency.

It was hoped that the new charges would serve a double purpose: first, to strengthen the charge of sedition; and, second, to reveal to Pilate that Jesus was a Galilean, because the Galileans were especially hated by the Romans, and by Pilate in particular. The mention of Galilee, however, had a far different effect on Pilate than was expected. "When Pilate heard of Galilee, he asked whether the Man was a Galilean. And as soon as he knew that He belonged unto Herod's jurisdiction, he sent Him to Herod, who himself also was at Jerusalem at that time." Luke 23:6, 7. The case had become embarrassing to the governor, and he gladly grasped the opportunity to shift the responsibility to another who was also his bitter enemy. Here was a way to get rid of a troublesome case without having to reverse his own decision.

Of this act of cowardice on the part of Pilate, Rosadi said: "This was the first of those unhappy subterfuges which Pilate resorted to in his desperate attempt to avoid the responsibilities of his office."—"*The Trial of Jesus*," *page 243*. Speaking of the efforts of the Roman judge to escape the responsibility of enforcing his decision, Chandler wrote: "Pilate showed himself throughout the trial a craven coward and contemptible timeserver. From beginning to end, his conduct was a record of cowardice and subterfuge. He was constantly looking for loopholes of escape. His heart's desire was to satisfy at once both his conscience and the mob. The mention of Galilee was a ray of light that fell across the troubled path of the cowardly and vacillating judge. He believed that he saw an avenue of escape. . . . He acted at once upon the happy idea; and, under the escort of a detachment of the praetorian cohort, Jesus was led away to the palace of the Maccabees where Herod was accustomed to stop when he came to the Holy City."—"*The Trial of Jesus*," *vol. 2, pp. 117, 118*.

The Character of Herod

Herod Antipas was the tetrarch of Galilee and Perea, and was also a visitor in Jerusalem during the Passover festival. His official residence was at Tiberias in Galilee. His position was that of a petty king under the Roman procurator; his authority, therefore, was very meager. During his visits to Jerusalem, Herod resided in the palace of the Maccabees, which was also located on Mount Zion near the palace of Herod where Pilate resided. "The old palace of the Asmoneans, in which Antipas lodged, was a short way from Pilate's splendid official residence. It lay a few streets off, to the northeast, within the same old city wall, on the slope of Zion, the leveled crest of which was occupied by the vast palace of Herod, now the Roman headquarters. . . . It was shortly after six, when Antipas, early astir, like all Orientals, heard the commotion in the courtyard of his palace, and received word that Jesus had been handed over to his authority. A few minutes more, and the prisoner was led into the court of justice of the palace, and presently Antipas made his appearance on the tribunal, on which Jesus was also forthwith placed."—*"The Life and Words of Christ," Geikie, page 763.*

Herod, dissolute and contemptible, was a Sadducean Jew, the son of Herod the Great, whose hands had been stained with the blood of nearly all his ten wives and of thousands of innocent victims. Antipas himself was the murderer of John the Baptist, who had dared to rebuke him for living unlawfully with his brother's wife. He probably had scarcely a spark of conscience or manhood left. Jesus was well acquainted with the character of His new judge. On one occasion Jesus had sent him a rebuke. Luke 13:31-33. Chandler says of Herod: "The pages of sacred history mention the name of no more shallow and contemptible character than this petty princeling, this dissolute Idumaean Sudducee. Compared with him, Judas is eminently respectable. Judas had a conscience which, when smitten with remorse, drove him to suicide. It is doubtful whether Herod had a spark of that celestial fire which we call conscience."—*"The Trial of Jesus," vol. 2, p. 120.*

"And when Herod saw Jesus, he was exceeding glad: for he was desirous to see Him of a long season, because he had heard many things of Him; and he hoped to have seen some miracle done by Him." Luke 23:8. Jesus was a Galilean, and had performed most of His mighty miracles in that country. For more than three years that entire region had been ringing with His praise and fame. Herod had been informed of these mighty works, but had never seen the Miracle Worker and was "exceeding glad" for the opportunity of meeting Him. He hoped that he and his court might be entertained with exhibitions of Christ's miracle-working power. The sick were therefore brought in and Jesus was commanded to heal them, with the promise of liberty as the reward.

Herod had no intention of condemning Jesus, who was very popular in Galilee; throughout his dominion Jesus was considered a prophet of God, and many believed Him to be the Messiah. Herod would not run the risk of a repetition of what had happened as the result of his murder of John the Baptist. He had lost enough popularity over that great blunder. He also believed that Jesus was either John the Baptist brought back to life or that God had raised up a greater prophet to take his place. "At that time Herod the tetrarch heard of the fame of Jesus, and said unto his servants, This is John the Baptist; he is risen from the dead; and therefore mighty works do show forth themselves in him." Matthew 14: 1, 2. "Now Herod the tetrarch heard of all that was done by Him: and he was perplexed, because that it was said of some, that John was risen from the dead; and of some, that Elias had appeared; and of others, that one of the old prophets was risen again. And Herod said, John have I beheaded: but who is this, of whom I hear such things? And he desired to see Him." Luke 9: 7-9. Herod would not run the risk of losing his position by incurring the wrath of his subjects. Later he did lose his crown because of the suspicions of Caligula, who had heard that Herod was conspiring against him.

"Then he questioned with Him in many words; but He answered him nothing." Luke 23:9. This was a fulfillment of Isaiah 53:7: "He was oppressed, and He was afflicted, yet He opened not His mouth: He is brought as a lamb to the slaughter, and as a sheep before her shearers is dumb, so He openeth not His mouth." The many questions of Herod were doubtless inspired by idle curiosity. "The murderer of prophets, who was living in open and flagrant incest, and who had no higher motive than mean curiosity, deserved no answer."—*The Cambridge Bible.* Jesus read the insincere motives of the wicked king, and gave him the severest rebuke possible—profound silence.

"The light, weak, crafty, worthless man was disposed to be very condescending. He put question after question to Him; whatever his idle curiosity suggested; and doubtless asked that a miracle might be performed there and then. But Jesus was no conjurer or 'magus.' He was ready to save His life by worthy means, but He would not, for a moment, stoop to anything unworthy. The creature clad in purple before Him was the murderer of John; the slave of a wicked woman, a mean adulterer. . . . Jesus felt, therefore, only utter disdain for him, and treated him with withering silence. He might tire himself with questions, but not a word of reply would be vouchsafed."—"*The Life and Words of Christ,*" *Geikie, pages 763, 764.* The silence of Jesus under the circumstances was the most eloquent testimony possible in defense of His innocence.

Another reason for the silence of Jesus was His knowledge that Herod had no legal jurisdiction over His case, as he was only a visitor in Jerusalem with no legal rights outside of Galilee.

During the entire time Jesus was before Herod the chief

dignitaries of the Jews continued their accusations. "The chief priests and scribes stood and vehemently accused Him." Luke 23: 10. They were doubtless getting worried for fear Herod would release Jesus, who they knew was capable of performing the miracles demanded of Him as the condition of acquittal. The Jews doubtless repeated all the charges they had brought against Jesus before Pilate, and had added those on which the Sanhedrin had found Him worthy of death. The religious charges would have weight with a Sadducean Jew, and they were therefore revived. The silence of Jesus was probably interpreted to Herod as an evidence of His guilt. The accusations of the Jews became more and more vehement as the evidence became clearer that Herod did not intend to pass judgment upon his Galilean subject. "They stood by while Herod quizzed Jesus, and when He refused to answer they broke loose with their accusations like a pack of hounds."—"*Word Pictures in the New Testament*," *A. T. Robertson, vol. 2, p. 280.*

Herod's Revenge

"And Herod with his men of war set Him at nought, and mocked Him, and arrayed Him in a gorgeous robe, and sent Him again to Pilate." Luke 23: 11. "Then, laughing to scorn the claims of Jesus, Herod (and his soldiers with him) made sport of Him, dressed Him in a gorgeous costume, and sent Him back to Pilate," is the rendering by Weymouth. The Greek original indicates that it was a bright or white robe, and many translators thus render it. Rosadi said: "Herod scoffed at Him for the small train of soldiers and courtiers which followed Him; clothed Him, out of mockery, in a garment of white and sent Him back to Pilate. . . . The white garment was the peculiar dress of illustrious persons; Tacitus even tells us that the tribunes were thus attired when they went before the eagles into battle. Perhaps the tetrarch had in mind the irony of this Roman custom."—"*The Trial of Jesus,*" *page 247.*

Pilate, as a Roman official, doubtless wore the white toga, and this act of Herod's was not only in mockery of Jesus, who claimed to be a king, but also a thrust at Pilate, his bitter enemy. Pilate later returned the thrust when he had Jesus arrayed in a purple robe, such as was worn by Herod as the evidence of his royalty. Notwithstanding these insinuating and insulting thrusts, Pilate and Herod, who had been enemies, became friends as the result of the experience. "The same day Pilate and Herod were made friends together: for before they were at enmity between themselves." Luke 23: 12.

The refusal of Herod to condemn Jesus was equivalent to an acquittal, and was so considered by Pilate. Luke 23: 13-16. "This involved a second distinct acquittal of our Lord from every political charge brought against Him. Had He in any way been guilty of either (1) perverting the people, (2) forbidding to pay tribute, or (3) claiming to be king, it would have been Herod's duty, and still more his interest, to punish Him. His dismissal of the case was a deliberate avowal of His innocence."—*The Cambridge Bible.*

Pilate told the Jews that he had found no fault in the prisoner, and that Herod also had come to the same conclusion. The judges of two separate tribunals had refused to ratify the Sanhedrin's sentence of death; instead, their examinations of the case had confirmed the innocence of the accused, and resulted in decisions for acquittal. The second announcement of the governor that the case was settled in favor of the prisoner brought keen disappointment to the Jews; but they were not yet ready to acknowledge defeat. They had dealt with Pilate before, and they knew that persistency and pressure would give them what they wanted. With a determination born of desperation, the Jewish rabble renewed the fight with a loud and united and insistent cry for vengeance upon the innocent victim of their wrath.

CHAPTER NINETEEN

CHRIST OR BARABBAS?

When Herod refused to condemn Jesus and returned Him to Pilate, the Roman governor was disappointed. He thought he had escaped the responsibility of dealing with the most embarrassing case in his experience as a judge. Addressing "the chief priests and the rulers and the people," he said: "Ye have brought this Man unto me, as one that perverteth the people: and, behold, I, having examined Him before you, have found no fault in this Man touching those things whereof ye accuse Him: no, nor yet Herod: for I sent you to him; and, lo, nothing worthy of death is done unto Him. I will therefore chastise Him, and release Him." Luke 23:13-16.

The suggestion of Pilate that in order to satisfy the demands of the mob, he would be willing to chastise one whom he had declared innocent was a base and cowardly proposal. "The proposal to scourge the prisoner was the second of those criminal and cowardly subterfuges through which Pilate sought at once to satisfy his conscience and the demands of the mob. . . . The injustice of this monstrous proposal was not merely contemptible, it was execrable. If Jesus was guilty, He should have been punished; if innocent, He should have been set free and protected from the assaults of the Jews."—*"The Trial of Jesus," Chandler, vol. 2, pp. 129, 130.* If Jesus were guilty of the crimes charged against Him, a mere chastising would not have been a sufficient punishment; but, if innocent, as the judge had just declared Him to be, any punishment whatever would be grossly unjust.

Of this second attempt on the part of Pilate to escape the responsibility of the case, The Cambridge Bible says: "Now was the golden opportunity which Pilate should have seized in order to do what he knew to be right; and he was really anxious to do it because the meek majesty of the Lord had made a deep impression upon him. . . . But men live under the coercion of their own past acts; and Pilate, by his cruelty and greed, had so bitterly offended the inhabitants of every province of Judea that he dared not do anything more to provoke the accusation which he knew to be hanging over his head. . . . This was the point at which Pilate began to yield to the fatal vacillation which soon passed into guilt and made it afterward impossible for him to escape. He had just declared the prisoner absolutely innocent. To subject Him, therefore, to the horrible punishment of scourging merely to gratify the pride of the Jews, and to humble Him in their eyes, was an act of disgraceful illegality which he must have felt to be most unworthy of the high Roman sense of 'justice.' The guilty dread which made Pilate a weak man is well illustrated by what Philo says of him."

Pilate Offers Barabbas

As if addressing the weak and vacillating judge as he wavered between justice and expediency, one writer said: "Be consistent with thyself, Pilate; for, if Christ is innocent, why dost thou not send Him away acquitted? And if thou believest Him deserving of chastisement with rods, why dost thou proclaim Him to be innocent?"—*Gerhard, Harm., ch. 193, p. 1889.* (*Greenleaf.*) But the rabble indignantly rejected the offer to compromise, and insistently demanded the death of their victim.

In his extremity, Pilate tried another scheme to rid himself of the responsibility of the case before him. There came to him as a happy thought a custom that had been inaugurated either by one of his predecessors or by Herod the Great. At the beginning of each Passover festival a prisoner, selected by the Jews themselves, was released by the procurator. "Now at that feast the governor was wont to release unto the people a prisoner, whom they would. And they had then a notable prisoner, called Barabbas. Therefore when they were gathered together, Pilate said unto them, Whom will ye that I release unto you? Barabbas, or Jesus which is called Christ? For he knew that for envy they had delivered Him. . . . But the chief priests and elders persuaded the multitude that they should ask Barabbas, and destroy Jesus. The governor answered and said unto them, Whether of the twain will ye that I release unto you? They said, Barabbas. Pilate saith unto them, What shall I do then with Jesus which is called Christ? They all say unto him, Let Him be crucified." Matthew 27: 15-22.

History tells us that this same custom prevailed at Athens and Rome. During great national festivals the people had the privilege of choosing a prisoner to be released by the authorities. It is quite probable, therefore, that the custom had been brought to Judea by the Romans. Josephus mentions this custom among the Jews, and, whatever its origin, it was so well established that it had become obligatory upon the procurator; "of necessity he must release one unto them at the feast." Luke 23: 17. At the time Pilate made the proposal it may be that groups of people were already arriving to make requests for the release of prisoners in whom they were especially interested, and it is only reasonable to suppose that considerable propaganda preceded the choice of the criminal to be pardoned. Petitions were doubtless circulated by friends and relatives of the various prisoners in the custody of the Romans.

The arrival of new people injected another element into the multitude, which gave the governor the hope that the great popularity of Jesus would bring about His release by the decision of the people in harmony with the prevailing Passover custom. He therefore reminded the Jews of the custom, and announced his readiness to set at liberty whom they would choose. Pilate felt quite certain that the populace would choose Jesus; but, to make such a choice more sure, he commanded the praetorium guards to bring from the prison the most dangerous and notorious criminal in custody. Placing him beside Jesus, he asked the rabble to decide between them.

In 1892 a copy of an ancient Syriac New Testament was discovered in the Convent of St. Catherine at Mount Sinai, in which the passage reads: "Which will ye that I release unto you, Jesus Bar Abba or Jesus that is called Christ?" This reading makes Pilate virtually say, "Which Jesus will you have, Jesus the son of Abba, or Jesus the King?" Jesus was on trial because He claimed to be the Messiah. Barabbas, or Bar Abba, was also called Jesus; and Jesus Barabbas meant "Jesus the son of Abba." Abba means "father;" therefore he was "Jesus the son of the father." He, too, had claimed to be the Messiah, and, in the effort to prove his claim and to establish his authority as the king of the Jews, he had instigated an insurrection in which there was considerable bloodshed. He was therefore awaiting sentence of death as a mover of sedition and as a murderer. "And there was one named Barabbas, which lay bound with them that had made insurrection with him, who had committed murder in the insurrection." Mark 15:7.

CHRIST OR BARABBAS?

Jesus Barabbas was guilty of the very things of which the Jews had falsely charged Jesus the Christ. A. T. Robertson says: "Barabbas was for some reason a popular hero, a notable, if not notorious, prisoner, leader of an insurrection or revolution probably against Rome, and so guilty of the very crime they tried to fasten on Jesus, who only claimed to be king in the spiritual sense of the spiritual kingdom. So Pilate unwittingly pitted against each other two prisoners who represented the antagonistic forces of all time."—"*Word Pictures in the New Testament,*" *Robertson, vol. 1, p. 225.*

THE TWO CLAIMANTS

As the two claimants for the Messiahship stood side by side on the porch of the praetorium, the contrast between them was so marked that it was evident to all who beheld them. Jesus had many friends who were attending the Passover, and doubtless some of them were in the new crowds that were arriving. The multitude would have chosen Jesus by acclamation had not the leaders of the Jews "persuaded the multitude that they should ask Barabbas, and destroy Jesus." Matthew 27: 20. To the surprise and chagrin of the governor, the multitude demanded the release of Barabbas the criminal, and the crucifixion of Jesus the Innocent. Regarding their choice, Peter later boldly said to the Jews: "Ye denied the Holy One and the Just, and desired a murderer to be granted unto you; and killed the Prince of life, whom God hath raised from the dead; whereof we are witnesses." Acts 3: 14, 15.

There was no longer any question in the mind of Pilate that the Jews were motivated by envy and hatred of Jesus. The cry, "Let Him be crucified," indicated that "there is no further question even of a show of legality or justice; the traditional clemency is quite forgotten; the fanatical crowd, pressing round the doors of the praetorium, which they cannot enter, join with excited gesticulation in one loud and furious cry for the blood of Jesus."—*The Cambridge Bible.* The wise man said that "jealousy is cruel as the grave." Canticles 8:6. He also asked, "Who is able to stand before envy?" Proverbs 27:4. Before the force of injustice inspired by jealousy and envy Pilate felt helpless and defeated.

While Pilate was wavering between duty and expediency, a messenger came out of the palace and handed him a message. It was from Claudia. "When he was set down on the judgment seat, his wife sent unto him, saying, Have thou nothing to do with that just Man: for I have suffered many things this day in a dream because of Him." Matthew 27:19. This warning filled Pilate with superstitious fear. Had not the wife of Julius Cæsar been warned in a dream of the fate awaiting him? She had implored her husband not to go to the Senate chamber in answer to the persistent urging of Brutus and his fellow conspirators; his assassination was the result of his failure to heed the warning. The Romans believed that the gods sent messages to men through dreams. Was this a warning from the gods of his fathers?

"Poor Pilate was getting more entangled every moment as he hesitated to set Jesus free, whom he knew to be free of any crime against Cæsar. Just at the moment when he was trying to enlist the people in behalf of Jesus against the schemes of the Jewish leaders, his wife sent a message about her dream concerning Jesus. She calls Jesus 'that righteous Man' and her physical sufferings increased Pilate's superstitious fears. . . . It was enough to unnerve the weak Pilate as he sat on the judgment seat."—"*Word Pictures in the New Testament,*" *Robertson, vol.* 1, *p.* 226.

The author of "The Desire of Ages" gives a graphic description of the dream that so alarmed Claudia: "In answer to Christ's prayer, the wife of Pilate had been visited by an angel from heaven, and in a dream she had beheld the Saviour and conversed with Him. Pilate's wife was not a Jew, but as she looked upon Jesus in her dream, she had no doubt of His character or mission. She knew Him to be the Prince of God. She saw Him on trial in the judgment hall. She saw the hands tightly bound as the hands of a criminal. She saw Herod and his soldiers doing their dreadful work. She heard the priests and rulers, filled with envy and malice, madly accusing. She heard the words, 'We have a law, and by our law He ought to die.' She saw Pilate give Jesus to the scourging, after he had declared, 'I find no fault in Him.' She heard the condemnation pronounced by Pilate, and saw him give Christ up to His murderers. She saw the cross uplifted on Calvary. She saw the earth wrapped in darkness, and heard the mysterious cry, 'It is finished.' Still another scene met her gaze. She saw Christ seated upon the great white cloud, while the earth reeled in space, and His murderers fled from the presence of His glory. With a cry of horror she awoke, and at once wrote to Pilate words of warning."—*Page 732.*

An Inspired Warning to Pilate

We can well imagine the consternation of Claudia when she awoke and learned that the very scenes of her dream were being enacted at the entrance of the praetorium and that her husband was the leading actor in the great drama of injustice. As the result of the warning, Pilate was determined if possible to escape the responsibility of convicting and crucifying an innocent man who might be more than a man.

It is a matter of historical record that provincial governors were required to report to the emperor from time to time the most important happenings under their administration. Tiberius was especially interested in trials and executions for treason, and it is more than probable that Pilate sent a somewhat detailed report to his master of the trial and crucifixion of Jesus, and one that would redound to his own glory. There are several apocryphal reports of this tragic event, but their authenticity is very doubtful.

While one could well imagine that the life and miracles of Jesus were included in the dream of Pilate's wife, it is not at all likely that the governor would render a report to his superior that would bring discredit upon himself. It is more reasonable to believe that if he sent a report of the trial and execution of the Christ, he would claim the credit for having put to death a traitor dangerous to the Roman Empire.

It is evident that the message of Claudia had a profound influence on Pilate's conduct during the remainder of the trial. The trial was thereby prolonged as the wavering and vacillating judge sought desperately for further subterfuges in order that he might escape from the fearful responsibility that had been imposed upon him by the Jewish authorities and the rabble that did their bidding. But all his efforts were in vain. He must face the ordeal, and eventually meet the results of his blunder. Justice always demands and obtains retribution for misconduct, and from this eventuality none can escape.

CHAPTER TWENTY

THE THREATENED APPEAL TO CÆSAR

THE warning from Claudia strengthened the determination of Pilate to escape the responsibility of condemning an innocent Man who might be what He claimed to be—more than a man. The governor knew that he could not set Jesus free without a compromise with the Jews. He must appease their wrath with some form of punishment. "Then Pilate therefore took Jesus, and scourged Him. And the soldiers platted a crown of thorns, and put it on His head, and they put on Him a purple robe, and said, Hail, King of the Jews! and they smote Him with their hands. Pilate therefore went forth again, and saith unto them, Behold, I bring Him forth to you, that ye may know that I find no fault in Him. Then came Jesus forth, wearing the crown of thorns, and the purple robe. And Pilate saith unto them, Behold the Man!" John 19: 1-5.

This was another cowardly attempt on the part of Pilate to save Jesus from the cross and at the same time save his own reputation. He hoped that the awful scourging would satisfy the enemies of Jesus, and excite their pity. This scourging was so terrible that the Jews limited the blows to "forty stripes save one." But Roman law did not restrict the number of lashes. The instrument of torture was a whip with a short handle to which were fastened several cords tipped with pieces of iron, lead, or bone. With each lash, these rough slugs partially buried themselves in the flesh of the victim. To make the scourging more effectual, the upper part of the body was made bare of clothing, and the prisoner was secured to a pillar or post with his arms around it and his hands tied together on the opposite side. So inhuman and brutal was a Roman scourging that death sometimes resulted from the terrible ordeal.

The lash of the scourge was sometimes applied to different parts of the body, including the face. It is evident from prophecy that Jesus was thus treated: "They shall smite the Judge of Israel with a rod upon the cheek." Micah 5: 1. The forecasts of the gospel prophet also indicate that the scourge was applied to the face of Jesus as well as to His back: "I gave My back to the smiters, and My cheeks to them that plucked off the hair: I hid not My face from shame and spitting." Isaiah 50: 6. The results of this treatment are described in Isaiah 52: 14: "As many were astonied at Thee; His visage was so marred more than any man, and His form more than the sons of men." "Many were appalled at His fate, kings shuddered at His doom," is the rendering by Moffatt.

But the soldiers were not through. In mockery to His claim to kingship, they conducted a mock court. A royal purple robe was thrown around the bruised and mutilated form of Jesus, and a wreath of cruel thorns, in the semblance of a crown, was placed upon His head. The soldiers then accorded Him mocking obeisance. They slapped Him on the face, plucked off His hair, jerked at His beard, and, as the insult of all insults, they spit in His face. In all human history no person ever suffered such indignities at the hands of men. Through it all Jesus maintained a dignified silence, and conducted Himself with a kingly bearing that astonished even His tormentors. They had never before witnessed such conduct on the part of a tortured prisoner.

It is evident that Jesus received this cruel treatment inside the praetorium or in one of its courts, and not in the presence of the Jews. After the scourging and mockery were over, Pilate "went forth again" to the Jews, and said, "Behold, I bring Him forth to you." John, who was present through the entire proceedings, declares: "Then came Jesus forth, wearing the crown of thorns, and the purple robe." John 19: 4, 5. The sight of the mutilated and suffering victim awakened pity even in the hearts of the cruel governor and his hardened soldiers, and Pilate brought Him out to the Jews, hoping that the scene might awaken at least a spark of sympathy in them. " 'Behold the Man!' This exclamatory introduction of Jesus in mock coronation robes to the mob was clearly intended to excite pity and to show how absurd the charge of the Sanhedrin was that such a pitiable figure should be guilty of treason. Pilate failed utterly in his effort, and did not dream that he was calling attention to the greatest figure of history, the Man of the ages."—"*Word Pictures in the New Testament*," *Robertson, vol. 5, p. 297.*

The Cambridge Bible declares that "Behold the Man!" was said "in pity rather than contempt. Pilate appeals to their humanity; surely the most bitter among them will now be satisfied, or at least the more compassionate will control the rest. No one can think that this Man is dangerous, or needs further punishment. When this appeal fails, Pilate's pity turns to bitterness." The sight of Jesus, with His robe and crown of mockery and His visage and form disfigured by the inhuman treatment He had just received, was enough to awaken pity if a spark of it existed in the Jews. Again Pilate declared Jesus to be innocent, and faultless. He indicated that he had already gone far beyond the law in the cruel treatment accorded the prisoner, with no other motive than to please and satisfy them. He hoped they would be considerate, and demand no further punishment of the One who had four times been declared guiltless. But his appeals fell on deaf ears, and the only response was a mighty shout demanding death by crucifixion. "When the chief priests therefore and officers saw Him, they cried out, saying, Crucify Him, crucify Him. Pilate saith unto them, Take ye Him, and crucify Him: for I find no fault in Him." John 19:6.

Religious Charge Revived

Pilate's challenge to the Jews to take the law into their own hands and crucify their own prisoner was met with a revival of the religious charge on which they had sentenced Jesus to die. "The Jews answered him, We have a law, and by our law He ought to die, because He made Himself the Son of God. When Pilate therefore heard that saying, he was the more afraid." John 19:7, 8. The repeated declaration of Pilate that Jesus was innocent of all criminal and political offenses charged against Him caused the Jews in their desperation to revive the indictment of blasphemy, which, according to Hebrew law, was a form of treason meriting the death penalty. This change in the indictment was an acknowledgment that the other charges were false, and that the real issue with them was a religious one.

The statement that Jesus ought to die because He claimed to be the Son of God filled Pilate with superstitious dread. It had the opposite effect than was intended by the Jews. In Roman mythology there were many legends of the sons of the gods visiting the earth in human form, and as such they were indistinguishable from mortal beings. To offend or to ill-treat these gods in the guise of men was a very serious offense, bringing down the anger of the gods. In

Acts 14: 11-15 is an example of this belief. The miracles of Paul and Barnabas convinced the people of Lystra that "the gods are come down to us in the likeness of men." The dream of Claudia doubtless came back vividly to the mind of Pilate, and he was more convinced than ever that Jesus was all He claimed to be.

To quiet his own fears and if possible to obtain a further explanation from Jesus as to His origin and mission, Pilate once again led Jesus back into the praetorium, on the pretense of investigating the new charges brought against Him. Pilate "went again into the judgment hall, and saith unto Jesus, Whence art Thou? But Jesus gave Him no answer. Then saith Pilate unto Him, Speakest Thou not unto me? knowest Thou not that I have power to crucify Thee, and have power to release Thee? Jesus answered, Thou couldest have no power at all against Me, except it were given thee from above: therefore he that delivered Me unto thee hath the greater sin." John 19: 9-11.

Jesus and Pilate

Jesus remained silent to the question of Pilate as to His origin. Pilate knew that Jesus was from Galilee, and had been reared in Nazareth. But this was not the information he was after. He was inquiring as to whether or not His claim of Sonship with God was true. Perhaps Jesus remained silent because an explanation could not have been understood by Pilate, and, anyway, His answer would have nothing to do with the merits of the case.

Pilate reminded Jesus that his supreme authority over Him demanded the courtesy of an answer, and that it would be to His advantage to honor him with a reply to his question; otherwise He might be guilty of contempt of court.

Jesus then reminded Pilate that his authority was restricted by a higher power, and that all governmental authority was delegated to man from above. He also told him that while he would be held responsible for his share of this travesty on justice, the greatest blame would rest upon the Jews, who delivered Him into his hands and were clamoring for His blood. This has been the judgment of mankind. With their greater light, the Jews must bear the greater guilt. Pilate greatly appreciated Jesus' statement that the Jews were the principal offenders in the crime being enacted against equity, and he was more determined than ever to release Him. The situation was becoming desperate, for the patience of both Pilate and the mob had reached the breaking point. Something must be done, and done quickly.

"From thenceforth Pilate sought to release Him: but the Jews cried out, saying, If thou let this Man go, thou art not Cæsar's friend: whosoever maketh himself a king speaketh against Cæsar. When Pilate therefore heard that saying, he brought Jesus forth, and sat down in the judgment seat in a place that is called the Pavement, but in the Hebrew, Gabbatha." John 19: 12, 13. Pilate was becoming disgusted with both himself and the rabble. He had decided to stop arguing, and to enforce his decree. He would no longer be made a fool of by the Jews, and he was on the verge of ordering them dispersed by the praetorium guards. Realizing what was about to happen, the Jews offered their final argument, which contained a threat of an appeal to Cæsar.

"The Jews once more shift their tactics, and from the ecclesiastical charge go back to the political, which they now back up by an appeal to Pilate's own political interests. They know their man; it is not a love of justice, but personal feelings which move him to seek to release Jesus; and they will overcome one personal feeling by another still stronger. Pilate's unexplained interest in Jesus and supercilious contempt for His accusers must give way before a fear for his own position, and possibly even his life. . . . The Jews perhaps scarcely knew how powerful their weapon was. Pilate's patron Sejanus (executed A. D. 31) was losing his hold over Tiberius, even if he had not already fallen. Pilate had already thrice nearly driven the Jews to revolt, and his character therefore would not stand high with an emperor who justly prided himself on the good government of the provinces. Above all, the terrible Lex Majestatis was by this time worked in such a way that prosecution under it was almost certain death."—*The Cambridge Bible.*

The threat of the Jews that they would appeal the case to Cæsar was not an idle one. They knew that a large delegation to Rome with the complaint that Pilate refused to execute one who claimed to be king, and was thus guilty of treason, would have great weight with suspicious Tiberius. They had appealed to the emperor on two or three previous occasions and got what they demanded, to the embarrassment of Pilate.

Pilate knew that such an appeal would cost him his position and probably his life, so the threat had the desired effect on the vacillating governor. He began to waver. The struggle had assumed a different aspect. It was no longer between justice and expediency so much as between justice and position, and position was dearer to Pilate than justice. He was now virtually on trial for his position and perhaps for his life. Either he or Jesus must be sacrificed, and he decided that he would save himself at the expense of the One who had five times been declared guiltless.

His respite, however, was short-lived, for a complaint of

the Jews a little later brought an order from the governor of Syria that Pilate appear before Tiberius to answer the serious charges against him. He was relieved of his office, and, according to Eusebius, "wearied with his misfortunes," he committed suicide. The oft-repeated saying of Jesus was thus fulfilled: "He that findeth his life shall lose it: and he that loseth his life for My sake shall find it." Matthew 10:39.

CHAPTER TWENTY-ONE

THE SENTENCE OF THE UNJUST JUDGE

THE threatened appeal to Cæsar weakened the determination of Pilate to release Jesus and to defend Him from the fury of the mob. He again began to parley with the Jews. Seating himself on the judgment seat in front of the praetorium, Pilate pointed to Jesus and in bitter irony said to the Jews, "Behold your King!" The answer of the mob was a unanimous demand that He be crucified. "They cried out, Away with Him, away with Him, crucify Him. Pilate saith unto them, Shall I crucify your King? The chief priests answered, We have no king but Cæsar. Then delivered he Him therefore unto them to be crucified. And they took Jesus, and led Him away." John 19: 14-16. Thus the Lord was sentenced to die.

In their desperation, the Jews were willing to acknowledge what they had always vehemently denied, that Cæsar was their only king. This was a virtual abandonment of the Messianic hope. In yielding to the clamor of the mob, Pilate proved his complete unfitness to act in the capacity of a Roman judge. The following well-established rule of Roman law was doubtless known to Pilate: "The idle clamor of the populace is not to be regarded, when they call for a guilty man to be acquitted, or an innocent one to be condemned."—*Law 12, Code de Poenis.* (*Greenleaf.*) "Poor mockery of a ruler! Set by the Eternal to do right on earth, and afraid to do it: told so by his own bosom: strong enough in his legions, and in the truth itself, to have saved the Innocent One, and kept his own soul—he could only think of the apparently expedient. Type of the politician of all ages, who forgets that only the right is the strong or wise!" —"*The Life and Words of Christ,*" *Geikie, page 767.*

Another of the four evangelists thus describes the final effort of Pilate to argue with the mob and the methods by which they forced him to acquiesce to their demands: "Pilate saith unto them, What shall I do then with Jesus which is called Christ? They all say unto him, Let Him be crucified. And the governor said, Why, what evil hath He done? But they cried out the more, saying, Let Him be crucified. When Pilate saw that he could prevail nothing, but that rather a tumult was made, he took water, and washed his hands before the multitude, saying, I am innocent of the blood of this just Person: see ye to it. Then answered all the people, and said, His blood be on us, and on our children. Then released he Barabbas unto them: and when he had scourged Jesus, he delivered Him to be crucified." Matthew 27: 22-26.

Of the attempt of Pilate to parley with the mob, Robertson has written: "This was a feeble protest by a flickering conscience. Pilate descended to that level of arguing with the mob now inflamed with passion for the blood of Jesus, a veritable lynching fiasco. . . . It was like a gladiatorial show with all thumbs turned down."—"*Word Pictures in the New Testament,*" *vol. 1, p. 227.* The final answer of the mob to the pleas of the Roman judge for justice was a "tumult." Webster defines a tumult as "the commotion or agitation of a multitude, usually with great uproar and confusion of voices." The arguments of Pilate were met with an uproar that drowned out his voice, and he gave up in despair and permitted them to have what they wanted.

Rosadi wrote regarding this scene: " 'Crucify Him!' was the last, unanimous, most piercing cry of the people, causing uproar in court. Not a single discordant voice was raised amidst the multitudinous clamor; not a word of protest disturbed the mighty concord of anger and reviling; not the faintest echo of the late hosannas, which had rung with wonder, fervor, and devotion, and which had surrounded and exalted to the highest pitch of triumph the bearer of good tidings on His entry into the Holy City. Where were the throngs of the hopeful and believing, who had followed His beckoning as a finger pointing towards the breaking dawn of truth and regeneration? Where were they, what thinking and why silent? . . . And the multitudes of disciples and enthusiasts who had scattered sweet-scented boughs and joyous utterances along the road to Sion, . . . where were they, what thinking and why silent? Not a remembrance, not a sign, not a word of the great glory so lately His."—"*The Trial of Jesus*," *pages 267, 268.*

How fickle is popular public opinion! How quickly the glad hosannas of the applauding multitude changed to the mad cry, "Crucify Him, crucify Him"! It seems that the more ardent and universal the acclamation, the more wild and unanimous the declamation when the tables begin to turn. Horace Greeley on his deathbed truthfully said: "Fame is vapor; popularity is an accident; riches take wings; they who cheer today may curse tomorrow. One thing endures—character." Jesus had the one thing that endures, and the passing centuries of time have enhanced rather than diminished His glory.

As a last resort, Pilate sought to escape the responsibility of his gross injustice by the performance of a theatrical act. "When Pilate saw that he could prevail nothing, but that rather a tumult was made, he took water, and washed his hands before the multitude, saying, I am innocent of the blood of this just Person: see ye to it. Then answered all the people, and said, His blood be on us, and on our children." Matthew 27: 24, 25.

Pilate's Symbolic Washing of Hands

To wash the hands of all responsibility in a matter had long been a custom among the Jews. See Deuteronomy 21: 6, 7; Psalms 26: 6; 73: 13. The custom was also not unknown to the Romans. "Not daring, in his weakness, to play the man, and do right, Pilate was yet determined that even those at a distance, who might not hear his disavowal of any willing share in the condemnation of Christ, should be made to see it. To wash the hands in water is a natural symbol, so expressive of repudiation of responsibility that it had been adopted by Jews and heathen alike."—"*The Life and Words of Christ,*" *Geikie, page 767.* The symbol has the same meaning at the present time.

Chandler wrote: "This was a simple, impressive, theatrical act; but little, mean, contemptible, cowardly. He washed his hands when he should have used them. He should have used them as Brutus or Gracchus or Pompeius Magnus would have done, in pointing his legion to the field of duty and of glory. He should have used them as Bonaparte did when he put down the mob in the streets of Paris. But he was too craven and cowardly; and herein is to be found the true meaning of the character and conduct of Pilate."—"*The Trial of Jesus,*" *vol. 2, pp. 137, 138.*

But Pilate could not so easily wash away his guilt. "The water did not wash away the blood of Jesus from his hands any more than Lady Macbeth could wash away the bloodstains from her lily-white hands."—"*Word Pictures in the New Testament,*" *Robertson, vol. 1, p. 228.* One writer declares that all the water of the Mediterranean would not have been sufficient to wash away the guilt of the Roman governor. He who repeatedly declared Jesus to be innocent and then sent Him to the cross has not been able to wash his hands of the matter, but has gone down in history as "the unjust judge."

Pilate Gave Sentence

"And they were instant with loud voices, requiring that He might be crucified. And the voices of them and of the chief priests prevailed. And Pilate gave sentence that it should be as they required." Luke 23:23, 24. "Thus ended the most memorable act of injustice recorded in history. At every stage of the trial, whether before Caiaphas or Pilate, the prisoner conducted Himself with that commanding dignity and majesty so well worthy of His origin, mission, and destiny. His sublime deportment at times caused His judges to marvel greatly. And through it all, He stood alone. His friends and followers had deserted Him in His hour of greatest need. Single-handed and unaided, the Galilean peasant had bared His breast and brow to the combined authority, to the insults and outrages, of both Jerusalem and Rome."—"*The Trial of Jesus,*" *Chandler, vol. 2, p. 139.* Through the prophet Isaiah, more than six centuries before, Christ had described this experience in the words: "I have trodden the wine press alone; and of the people there was none with Me." Isaiah 63:3. His great popularity had vanished, and He was left alone.

That the sentence of death which sent Jesus to the cross after He had so many times been declared innocent was nothing short of judicial murder is the verdict of mankind. The previously quoted legal authority says: "The pages of human history present no stronger case of judicial murder than the trial and crucifixion of Jesus of Nazareth, for the simple reason that all forms of law were outraged and trampled underfoot in the proceedings instituted against Him. The errors were so numerous and the proceedings so flagrant that many have doubted the existence of a trial."—*Id., vol. 1, p. 216.* The noted Italian advocate says that "the governor did not summon a single witness, did not verify any evidence, did not set before himself any investigation as to innocence or guilt, nay, . . . he was satisfied as to the innocence of the prisoner, and yet decided in favor of guilt and condemnation."—"*The Trial of Jesus,*" *Rosadi, pages 236, 237.*

Rosadi sums up this greatest travesty on justice as follows: "Thus ended the trial before the praetorium. But the name of trial is ill-befitting to the chain of wild, savage, and disorderly proceedings which followed one upon another from early morning. . . . Jesus was now condemned. That He was tried cannot be said, for who were His judges and when did they judge Him? Not they of the Sanhedrin, for they had not the power, nor did they claim it. Not by the Roman magistrate in the praetorium, who heard no single word of evidence, sought not a single proof, weighed not a single pleading, observed not a single form. Were one to forget the place of the proceeding—a Roman tribunal—were one to forget the date, some eight centuries after the foundation of the city of Rome, that had no childhood—Rome, the teacher of law to civilized mankind—one might imagine that one was present at some primitive trial taking place before the curule throne of one of the first Roman kings without the slightest guarantee of even the most grotesque ritual forms. But at the time when these things took place, the law-giving genius of Rome had reached, in the organization of its criminal tribunals, the highest pinnacle of civilization."—*Id., page 288.*

The Slain Lamb

Prophecy declared that Jesus would be "brought as a lamb to the *slaughter*." Isaiah 53:7. It was therefore predicted long before that His death would be a *slaughter* rather than the execution of a legal sentence. The apostle Peter on the day of Pentecost told the Jews that they were guilty of the murder of the Son of God. He said: "Him, being delivered by the determinate counsel and foreknowledge of God, ye have taken, and by wicked hands have crucified and *slain*." Acts 2:23. On a later occasion Peter and the other apostles said to the Jews: "The God of our fathers raised up Jesus, whom ye *slew* and hanged on a tree." Acts 5:30. The angelic host and the multitudes of the redeemed will sing throughout all eternity of "the Lamb that was *slain*." See Revelation 5:9, 12.

Not only is it the judgment of the world that Jesus was *slain* rather than executed, but modern advocates who have carefully reviewed the case have also declared that the crucifixion of Jesus constituted *murder*. Rosadi says: "There was neither inscription nor even definition of the charge; the crime was not formally declared; no appropriate legal enactment was applied; there was no hearing of witnesses; there was no proof of a criminal act; there was nothing said in justification or explanation of the sentence. There was in fact no sentence; the prisoner was merely handed over by a motion of the hand of His accusers, in open contrast to the proclamation of the judge who had declared the innocence of the Accused and had then washed his hands of the matter.

Jesus of Nazareth was not condemned, but He was slain. His martyrdom was no miscarriage of justice, it was a murder."—Id., page 294. (Italics mine.) Thus was Isaiah 59: 14-16 completely and strikingly fulfilled.

CHAPTER TWENTY-TWO

THE CRUCIFIXION

"And so Pilate, willing to content the people, released Barabbas unto them, and delivered Jesus, when he had scourged Him, to be crucified." Mark 15: 15. We know from the records of history that it was a Roman custom to scourge condemned criminals before the sentence of death was executed. This was considered a part of the deserved punishment. The following passages are taken from the "Antiquities" of Josephus: "Whom, having first scourged with whips, he crucified." "Being beaten, they were crucified opposite to the citadel." "He was burned alive, having first been beaten." Livy, a Roman historian of the first century, tells of an execution in the following sentence: "All were led out, beaten with rods, and beheaded."—*Lib. XI, c. 5.*

It was also the custom of the time to turn condemned criminals over to the soldiers and the populace for torment, mockery, and ridicule, as a part of their punishment. Of this humiliating experience Jesus received more than the usual portion. Three times was Jesus buffeted and persecuted in this manner: by the Jews, by the soldiers of Herod, and by the soldiers of Pilate. In these things the testimony of the Gospel writers coincides with collateral circumstances and contemporary writers, and thus meets one of the most important tests of credibility. This is true of every part of their writings. Said Tacitus, the Roman historian: "To the sufferings of those who were put to death were added mockery and derision."—"*Annals*," *XV, 44.*

It was also the custom of the time for the victim to carry his own cross to the place of execution. This practice was followed in the crucifixion of Jesus. "Then delivered he Him therefore unto them to be crucified. And they took Jesus, and led Him away. And He bearing His cross went forth into a place called the place of a skull, which is called in the Hebrew Golgotha: where they crucified Him, and two other with Him, on either side one, and Jesus in the midst." John 19:16-18. Of this ancient practice, Plutarch, a Greek historian of the first century, says: "Every kind of wickedness produces its own particular torment; just as every malefactor, when he is brought forth to execution, carries his own cross."—"*De iis qui sero puniuntur*," *page 554.*

Since Jesus died in *our* stead, the cross on which He died was really *our* cross. We, the sinners, are guilty of death. Jesus met the penalty of the broken law on our behalf. "He was wounded for our transgressions, He was bruised for our iniquities." "And the Lord hath laid on Him the iniquity of us all." It was therefore *our* cross that Jesus carried and on which He was crucified.

Jesus fell under the weight of the heavy cross, and it had to be laid on the shoulders of another, who, as the result of the experience, became an ardent disciple. The humiliating experience was a blessing in disguise. Just as Simon, the Cyrenian, bore the cross "after Jesus," so to every disciple Jesus says: "He that taketh not his cross, and followeth after Me, is not worthy of Me." Matthew 10:38.

In the procession that followed Jesus to Golgotha were many women who "bewailed and lamented Him." Jesus turned to them and said: "Daughters of Jerusalem, weep not for Me, but weep for yourselves, and for your children. For, behold, the days are coming, in the which they shall say, Blessed are the barren, and the wombs that never bare, and the paps which never gave suck. Then shall they begin to say to the mountains, Fall on us; and to the hills, Cover us. For if they do these things in a green tree, what shall be done in the dry?" Luke 23:28-31.

What did Jesus mean by this statement? His prediction of coming calamity was partly fulfilled in the destruction of Jerusalem by the Romans, but it will meet its final and complete fulfillment at His second advent. Revelation 6:14-17. Jesus declared that if He, the green and fruitful tree, was so unjustly treated, what would be the fate of Israel, a dry, dead, leafless, and barren tree? A green tree cut down may sprout again, but a dry tree perishes forever. He would live again, but the nation that rejected and crucified Him would never be restored.

The Place "Golgotha"

The place where Jesus was crucified is called Calvary in Latin, and Golgotha in Hebrew. The Greek is *Kranion*. The name means "skull," and is spoken of as "the place of a skull." It was not a place of skulls, as some suppose, but rather a place that resembled a skull because of the shape of the summit of the hill. North of Jerusalem is what is known as "Gordon's Calvary," which, seen from the wall of the city, somewhat resembles a skull, with two caves below the brow suggesting eyes. While we are told that the place "was nigh to the city," the exact location can only be a matter of conjecture.

According to Mark 15:25, Jesus was crucified at "the third hour," or nine o'clock in the morning. Two thieves were crucified at the same time, one on either side of Him. Thus was fulfilled the prediction of the prophet that "He was numbered with the transgressors."

Before being crucified, Jesus was stripped of His outer

garments, which probably consisted of a cloak, a sort of shirt, a girdle, and a pair of sandals. The soldiers divided these among themselves, casting lots over them. "They crucified Him, and parted His garments, casting lots: that it might be fulfilled which was spoken by the prophet, They parted My garments among them, and upon My vesture did they cast lots." Matthew 27:35. The prophecy quoted is from Psalm 22:18. This, too, was a Roman custom, and the record of it constitutes another evidence of the credibility of the account.

Just before Jesus was nailed to the cross He was offered the "death draught": "They gave Him vinegar to drink mingled with gall: and when He had tasted thereof, He would not drink." Matthew 27:34. This also was a fulfillment of prophecy. See Psalm 69:21. The drink offered Jesus was a mixture of frankincense and myrrh poured into a cup of vinegar. Its purpose was to produce stupefaction in order to render the victim partially unconscious to the pain caused by the nails. This was a Hebrew custom sponsored by wealthy Jewish women of Jerusalem. Lightfoot declares that "some of the wealthy ladies of Jerusalem charged themselves with this office of mercy."

Accusation in Writing

"Pilate wrote a title, and put it on the cross. And the writing was, JESUS OF NAZARETH THE KING OF THE JEWS. This title then read many of the Jews: for the place where Jesus was crucified was nigh to the city: and it was written in Hebrew, and Greek, and Latin." John 19:19, 20. This inscription contained the name of the condemned, His place of residence, and the charge on which He was sentenced to be crucified. Matthew declared that the inscription was "set up over His head." It was doubtless nailed to the top of the upright beam of the cross. The accusation was written in the three leading languages spoken in Palestine, so that all could read it. Hebrew was the national dialect of the Jews; Greek was the universal tongue of the civilized world; and Latin was the official language of the judicial and executive power of the then ruling world empire. Geikie declares that the three languages were a symbol of "the relation of the cross to all the nationalities of the world."

This act of Pilate was also a well-established Roman custom. Suetonius, a Roman historian of the first century, describes an execution by order of Domitian as follows: "He exposed the father of the family to the dogs, with this title, 'A gladiator, impious in speech.' " The victim was the father of a family who had spoken disrespectfully of a fellow gladiator. Dion Cassius, a Greek-Roman historian of the second century, described a crucifixion scene thus: "Having led him through the midst of the court or assembly, with a writing signifying the cause of his death, and afterward crucifying him." On such occasions the placard was either carried before the victim or hung around his neck. Again the New Testament record bears the acid test of concurring with the current customs of the time and of the testimony of contemporary writers.

The Instrument of Torture

It is said that the use of the cross as an instrument of punishment had its origin in the ancient practice of fastening a criminal "to a tree, which was termed 'accursed,' " and was later known as "the cross." The cross was therefore still spoken of as a "tree" in the days of the apostles.

Peter wrote: "Who His own self bare our sins in His own body on the tree, that we, being dead to sins, should live unto righteousness: by whose stripes ye were healed." 1 Peter 2: 24. The cross as first used by the Babylonians during the reign of Semiramis was in the form of a T, for Tammuz, one of the names of Nimrod, her husband.

The modern conceptions of the cross on which Jesus was crucified are far from the facts of history; and pictorial art must bear the brunt of the blame. No man could possibly have carried the cross as usually pictured with the victim hanging so high above the earth that a ladder must be used to reach him. Of the historical cross used by the Romans, Chandler writes: "The pictures of crosses in works of art are misrepresentations, in that they are too large and too high. The real cross of antiquity was very little longer than the victim, whose head was near the top, and whose feet often hung only twelve or fifteen inches from the ground. Pictorial art is also false because it fails to show the projecting beam from near the center of the cross upon which the criminal sat. That there was such a beam is attested by the almost unanimous voice of antiquity."—*"The Trial of Jesus," vol. 2, p. 56.*

Of the ancient cross, Renan wrote: "A piece of wood was fastened to the upright portion of the cross, toward the middle, and passed between the legs of the condemned, who rested upon it. Without that, the hands would have been torn and the body would have sunk down. At other times, a small horizontal rest was fixed beneath the feet, and sustained them."—*"The Life of Jesus," page 364.* Irenaeus, one of the early church fathers, said: " 'The structure of the cross has five ends or summits, two in length, two in breadth, and one in the middle, on which the crucified person rests.' "

Justin Martyr mentioned a projecting end from the middle of the upright post " 'like a horn, on which crucified persons are seated,' " and Tertullian wrote of " 'the projecting bar which serves as a seat.' " Stroud described the cross as "having a short bar or stake projecting from its middle."—"*The Physical Cause of the Death of Christ*," *pages 35, 36.*

A few years ago a German artist painted some pictures of the crucifixion of Jesus with the cross of the size and construction in universal use in Christ's time. But they were so unpopular that the public practically rejected them. The majority of the people of the modern world prefer something that is false if it makes a greater appeal to their fancy. Of course, the size and structure of the cross are only minor incidentals compared with the meaning and significance of the crucifixion itself. The death of Christ on the cross of Calvary is the greatest event of all history.

CHAPTER TWENTY-THREE

SUFFERINGS OF JESUS ON THE CROSS

JESUS was crucified at nine o'clock in the morning, and died at three in the afternoon. He thus spent six hours on the cross before death ended His sufferings. Beginning at noon, and continuing until His death, a blanket of thick darkness enveloped the cross and veiled the sufferer from the gaze of the multitude. "And it was about the sixth hour, and there was a darkness over all the earth until the ninth hour. And the sun was darkened, and the veil of the temple was rent in the midst." Luke 23:44, 45.

When the thief turned to Christ with the request, "Lord, remember me when Thou comest into Thy kingdom," immediately the answer came back from the central cross: "You ask to be remembered then, verily thou art assured now. Thou shalt be with Me in Paradise." Luke 23:39-43, Rotherham. The thief did not ask to be remembered before the rewarding time at the second advent, when the kingdom of glory would be ushered in, and Christ did not promise him a place in Paradise until then. Jesus made the promise the very day when the fulfillment of His word seemed impossible. When the comma is shifted to its proper place in the Authorized Version,—all punctuation, as is well known, came into use in later times,—the meaning is clear: "Verily I say unto thee today, shalt thou be with Me in Paradise." The promise was made that day; its fulfillment was a future event. In fact, the scriptural record makes it plain that Jesus Himself did not go to Paradise that day. On the morning of His resurrection He told Mary that He had not yet ascended to His Father. John 20:16, 17. According to Revelation 2: 7; 22: 1-5, Paradise is where God's throne is. The request of the repentant thief was the only human recognition of the identity and mission of Jesus during the entire period of His sufferings, and this experience did much to strengthen His faith and courage for the struggle before Him.

The Physical Sufferings of Crucifixion

Drawing his information from the records of history and medical science, Geikie gives the following graphic description of the physical tortures accompanying death by crucifixion: "The suffering in crucifixion, from which death at last resulted, rose partly from the constrained and fixed position of the body, and of the outstretched arms, which caused acute pain from every twitch or motion of the back, lacerated by the knout, and of the hands and feet, pierced by the nails. These latter were, moreover, driven through parts where many sensitive nerves and sinews come together, and some of these were mutilated, others violently crushed down. Inflammation of the wounds in both hands and feet, speedily set in, and erelong rose also in other places, where the circulation was checked by the tension of the parts. Intolerable thirst, and ever-increasing pain, resulted. The blood, which could no longer reach the extremities, rose to the head, swelled the veins and arteries in it unnaturally, and caused the most agonizing tortures in the brain. As, besides, it could no longer move freely from the lungs, the heart grew more and more oppressed, and all the veins were distended. Had the wounds bled freely, it would have been a great relief, but there was very little lost. The weight of the body itself, resting on the wooden pin of the upright beam; the burning heat of the sun scorching the veins, and the hot wind, which dried up the moisture of the body, made each moment more terrible than that before. The numbness and stiffness of the more distant muscles brought on painful convulsions, and this numbness, slowly extending, sometimes through two or three days, at last reached the vital parts, and released the sufferer by death."—"*The Life and Words of Christ*," *pages* 781, 782.

Dr. Richter, a celebrated physician, discussed the pathological phases of death by crucifixion. From his treatise the following has been reproduced in McClintock and Strong's "Cyclopedia of Biblical, Theological, and Ecclesiastical Literature," vol. 2, page 590:

"1. The unnatural position and violent tension of the body, which cause a painful sensation from the least motion.

"2. The nails, being driven through parts of the hands and feet which are full of *nerves* and *tendons* create the most exquisite anguish.

"3. The exposure of so many wounds and lacerations brings on inflammation, which tends to become gangrene, and every moment increases the poignancy of the suffering.

"4. In the distended parts of the body more blood flows through the arteries than can be carried back into the veins: hence too much blood finds its way from the aorta into the head and stomach, and the blood vessels of the head become pressed and swollen. The general obstruction of circulation which ensues causes an internal excitement, exertion, and anxiety more intolerable than death itself.

"5. The inexpressible misery of *gradually increasing* and lingering anguish. . . .

"6. Burning and raging thirst.

"Death by crucifixion is therefore to be attributed to the sympathetic fever which is excited by the wounds, and aggravated by exposure to the weather, privation of water, and the painfully constrained position of the body. Traumatic fever corresponds, in intensity and in character, to the local inflammation of the wound. In the first stage, while the inflammation of the wound is characterized by heat, swelling, and great pain, the fever is highly inflammatory, and the sufferer complains of heat, throbbing headache, intense thirst, restlessness, and anxiety. . . . If the wound be prevented from healing, and suppuration continue, the fever assumes a hectic character, and will sooner or later exhaust the powers of life. When, however, the inflammation of the wound is so intense as to produce mortification, nervous depression is the immediate consequence; and if the cause of this excessive inflammation of the wound still continues, as is the case in crucifixion, the sufferer rapidly sinks. He is no longer sensible of pain, but his anxiety and sense of prostration are excessive; hiccough supervenes, his skin is moistened with a cold clammy sweat, and death ensues. It is in this manner that death on the cross must have taken place in an ordinarily healthy constitution."

Suffered Many Tortures

That Jesus suffered many of the tortures here described is evident, even though His death occurred only six hours after He was nailed to the cross. Crucified persons usually lived two or three days, and at times a week or more. The longer they lived, of course the greater the physical sufferings. The sensitive and refined nature of Jesus, however, must have greatly augmented His physical tortures, so that the six hours were more terrible than two or three days to a hardened criminal. The cry of Jesus, "I thirst," was said not only to fulfill the prophecy, "in My thirst they gave Me vinegar to drink" (Psalm 69: 21), but it was also an indication that inflammation had already produced that fever which is always accompanied by a burning thirst.

As terrible as were His physical sufferings, Jesus was tortured by a greater mental anguish. "About the ninth hour Jesus cried with a loud voice, saying, Eli, Eli, lama sabachthani? that is to say, My God, My God, why hast Thou forsaken Me?" Matthew 27: 46. As the sinner's substitute, Jesus had to experience the feelings of utter God-abandonment that will come to every lost sinner. He was passing through that horror of great darkness in which not even one ray of hope pierces the gloom. He felt to the full that unutterable anguish accompanying the sense of complete and eternal separation from God because of sin. It was on the cross that the Son of God felt to the limit the crushing weight of the sins of the whole world. If His sufferings had consisted in physical pain alone, His death would have been far less painful than that of many of the martyrs. But bodily pain was only a very small part of His agony.

Not only was the anguish of Jesus intensified by the weight of the sins of guilty man, but worse still was the sense of His Father's wrath as He suffered in man's stead the penalty of the broken law. The hiding of His Father's face brought to Christ the feeling that He was forsaken by the One nearest and dearest to Him, and His despair was indescribably terrible. He keenly felt the results of the separation that sin makes between God and man. The martyrs all died with the consciousness of acceptance with God, and therefore their death bears no comparison to that of Jesus as He bore the agonies of the cross of Calvary. It was this that wrung from the lips of the suffering Messiah the bitter cry, "My God, My God, why hast Thou forsaken Me?"

SUFFERINGS OF JESUS ON THE CROSS

Dr. David Russell declares that on the cross the Gethsemane struggle of Jesus, which had been temporarily abated by the visit of the angel, was resumed and carried to its tragic climax: "On the cross the scene of Gethsemane was renewed; the cup was again presented to Him, and there He drank it to the very dregs. On Calvary His distress reached its height, and drew from Him the bitter exclamation, 'My God, My God, why hast Thou forsaken Me?' Mysterious dereliction! only to be accounted for by the nature of His death. . . . He at last expired under the curse, not so much in consequence of the exhaustion of nature by bodily pain and the loss of blood, . . . as in consequence of the extreme pressure of mental torture. This was too racking, too exquisite for nature to support—it literally broke His heart."—*"Letters, Chiefly Practical and Consolatory," vol. 1, p. 79. (Stroud.)*

Death came as a sweet release to the physical and mental sufferings of Jesus, but not before the impenetrable gloom lifted and He was given the assurance of His Father's love and acceptance. He had gone into the very depths of despair in paying the redemption price for guilty man, so that justice was fully satisfied. As His heart was breaking under the terrible strain, a ray of light broke through the darkness, and with His dying breath He was able to say, "Father, into Thy hands I commend My spirit." Luke 23:46. He died with the knowledge that He had finished His earthly mission, conquered the power of sin, and provided a way of escape for guilty man. The cry, "It is finished," the shout of a conqueror, resounded throughout the universe. The triumphant death of Christ vindicated the government of God, and "with one voice the loyal universe united in extolling the divine administration."

CHAPTER TWENTY-FOUR

DIED OF A BROKEN HEART

PROPHECY declared that the Messiah would die as the result of a broken, or ruptured, heart. The fortieth Psalm is a Messianic prophecy, and in verse twelve we are told of the "innumerable evils" that would encompass Him during His earthly pilgrimage, climaxing in His death, the cause of which is given in the statement, "Therefore My heart faileth Me." The sixty-ninth Psalm gives the meditations of Jesus while on the cross, in which is a forecast of the cause of His death: "Reproach hath broken My heart; and I am full of heaviness: and I looked for some to take pity, but there was none; and for comforters, but I found none. They gave me also gall for My meat; and in My thirst they gave Me vinegar to drink." Verses 20, 21.

From the account of the death of Jesus it is evident that His sudden decease was the result of a ruptured heart. "The peculiar atrocity of crucifixion was that one might live three or four days in this horrible state upon the instrument of torture. The hemorrhage from the hands quickly stopped, and was not mortal. The true cause of death was the unnatural position of the body, which brought on a frightful disturbance of the circulation, terrible pains of the head and heart, and, at length, rigidity of the limbs. Those who had a strong constitution only died of hunger. . . . Everything leads to the belief that the instantaneous rupture of a vessel in the heart brought Him . . . to a sudden death."—*"The Life of Jesus," Renan, pages 367, 368.*

That Jesus died of a broken heart is also the opinion of Geikie: "The immediate cause of death appears, beyond question, to have been the rupture of His heart, brought about by mental agony."—*"The Life and Words of Christ," page 788.* There can be no question but that Jesus lived in harmony with the laws of nature, and therefore must have had a more than ordinarily strong physical constitution. Under ordinary circumstances, He should have lived several days on the cross before death ended His agony.

The Weight of Sin Upon the Saviour

Another well-known writer thus describes the death of Christ: "In yielding up His precious life, Christ was not upheld by triumphant joy. All was oppressive gloom. It was not the dread of death that weighed upon Him. It was not the pain and ignominy of the cross that caused His inexpressible agony. . . . With the terrible weight of guilt He bears, He cannot see the Father's reconciling face. The withdrawal of the divine countenance from the Saviour in this hour of supreme anguish pierced His heart with a sorrow that can never be fully understood by man. So great was this agony that His physical pain was hardly felt. . . . It was the sense of sin, bringing the Father's wrath upon Him as man's substitute, that made the cup He drank so bitter, and broke the heart of the Son of God."—*"The Desire of Ages," pages 752, 753.*

Besides the forecasts of prophecy, there are several evidences in the nature of the death of Jesus that show that He died of a broken heart. It is proved in the first place by the fact that death occurred so soon after He was crucified. When Joseph of Arimathaea went to Pilate and asked for the privilege of burying Jesus, we are told that "Pilate marveled if He were already dead: and calling unto him the centurion, he asked him whether He had been any while dead." Mark 15: 44. It was almost an unheard-of thing for a crucified person to die within two or three days unless death was hastened by other means. It is evident, therefore, that Jesus did not die as the result of the crucifixion itself. In the second place, Jesus died very suddenly in the midst of terrible agony of mind and spirit. There was apparently no evidence that death was near when His life was suddenly and unexpectedly terminated. Crucifixion always caused a long, slow, and lingering death, in which the victim grew weaker and weaker until he became unconscious.

A Rupture of the Heart

In the third place, the death of Jesus immediately followed a loud and piercing cry. Matthew 27: 50; Luke 23: 46. Usually, in case of death, the voice is the first faculty to fail. It grows weaker and fainter until it becomes inaudible. The loud and piercing cry of Jesus indicated great physical strength, which could suddenly be terminated only by the rupture of the heart. An eminent physician declared that when a person dies of heart rupture "the hand is suddenly carried to the front of the chest, and a piercing shriek uttered." Jesus, of course, could not move His hands because they were nailed to the cross. The fourth and most convincing evidence of all that Jesus died of heart rupture was the flow of blood and water from the wound made in His side by the thrust of the soldier's spear. "One of the soldiers with a spear pierced His side, and forthwith came there out blood and water. And he that saw it bare record, and his record is true: and he knoweth that he saith true, that ye might believe." John 19: 34, 35.

Medical science has not only recorded many cases in which sudden death was the result of heart rupture caused by excessive grief, extreme anguish, or violent passion, but that, when the heart of a person who has so died is suddenly punctured, coagulated blood and a waterlike substance, or serum, flows out, sometimes in large quantities.

Dr. William Stroud, an eminent physician of England and Scotland, gathered much evidence along this line and included it in his book entitled "The Physical Cause of the Death of Christ," to which reference has been made in preceding pages. He quotes a Dr. C. D. Ludwig, who describes a case of rupture of the right auricle of the heart: " 'The pericardium was so distended by a large quantity of transparent serum and coagulated blood, as to push the lungs upwards. The yellowish serum contained in its cavity exceeded half a pound. The heart was encompassed by much clotted blood, which adhered to it on all sides, and was perceived to have escaped slowly through a fissure detected in the margin of the right auricle.' " Dr. Stroud states that "from the researches of Lancisi, Ramazzini, Morgagni, and other anatomists, it appears that a quart of blood, and sometimes much more, might thus be collected in the pericardium, where it would speedily separate into its solid and liquid constituents, technically called crassamentum and serum, but in ordinary language,—'blood and water.' "—*Pages 127, 143.*

The doctor cites another case where "a small rupture was found in the left ventricle of the heart; and the pericardium was so distended as to occupy a third part of the cavity of the chest. On opening it, a large quantity of serum was discharged, and two pounds of clotted blood were seen adhering at the bottom." The London *Medical Repository* for 1814 is quoted as reporting a sudden death from the rupture of an aneurism of the aorta. " 'The sac had burst by an aperture of nearly three fourths of an inch in length into the pericardium, which, as well as the sac itself, was filled with coagula [clots or curds] and serum, to the amount of about five pounds.'" The London *Medical and Physical Journal* for May, 1822, is mentioned as recording another case where "'the pericardium, which appeared much distended, had a bluish color, and presented an evident degree of fluctuation, contained a quantity of serum and coagulated blood.'" The same journal of April, 1826, reported a case where "the pericardium was found to be distended with blood; separated however into coagulum and serum." —*Id., pages 150, 151.*

The same physician quotes a Dr. Ollier's description of a case where "'the pericardium contained about a quart of blood and water. The blood was separated, although indistinctly, into serum and crassamentum [a clot, as of blood].'" Another physician cites a case of heart rupture where the right pleural sac "contained a great quantity of clear serum, intermixed with large coagula of blood, the whole effusion amounting to full five pints." The Edinburgh *Medical and Surgical Journal* for January, 1843, is cited as recording a case in which "'the cavity of the right pleura was found to be almost filled with blood, which had separated into serum and crassamentum; the former amounted to three pints, and the coagulated portion, which was exceedingly firm, weighed about three pounds.'"—*Id., page 152.*

Dr. Stroud thus sums up the evidence he had collected from medical authorities: "In conclusion, it may therefore with certainty be affirmed, that between the agony of mind which the Saviour endured in the Garden of Gethsemane, and the profuse sweat mixed with clotted blood which so rapidly followed it, violent palpitation of the heart must necessarily have intervened; this being the only known condition which could have been at once the effect of the former occurrence, and the cause of the latter. . . . If, whilst every other explanation hitherto offered has been shown to be untenable, the cause now assigned for the death of Christ, namely, RUPTURE OF THE HEART FROM AGONY OF MIND, has been proved to be the result of an actual power in nature, fully adequate to the effect, really present without counteraction, minutely agreeing with all the facts of the case, and necessarily implied by them, this cause must, according to the principles of inductive reasoning, be regarded as demonstrated."—*Id., pages 155, 156.*

"The Jews therefore, because it was the preparation, that the bodies should not remain upon the cross on the Sabbath day, (for that Sabbath day was an high day,) besought Pilate that their legs might be broken, and that they might be taken away. Then came the soldiers, and brake the legs of the first, and of the other which was crucified with him. But when they came to Jesus, and saw that He was dead already, they brake not His legs." John 19: 31-33.

Another Roman Custom

The historical records of those times tell us that the legs of crucified prisoners were sometimes broken in order to hasten death so that the soldiers would not have to remain on guard so long. The guards were generally ordered to remain till the victims died, so as to prevent friends or relatives from taking them down from the cross. There are recorded instances of this having been done, and of the recovery of the victim.

Punishment by crucifixion was abolished by edict of

Constantine after his nominal conversion to Christianity. The historian says: "He thought it indecent and irreligious that the cross should be used for the punishment of the vilest offenders, whilst he himself erected it as a trophy, and esteemed it the noblest ornament of his diadem, and military standards. . . . The same religious sentiment induced Constantine likewise to forbid breaking the legs of criminals, a punishment often annexed to that of the cross."—*"History of the Roman Emperors," J. B. L. Crevier, vol. 10, p. 132. (Stroud.)* An ancient writer said of Constantine: "He was pious to such a degree, that he was the first to set aside that very ancient punishment, the cross, and the breaking of legs." See also Paley's "View of the Evidences of Christianity," pages 266-268. It had been divinely ordered that the bones of the sacrificial victims, which were symbolic of the antitypical Lamb of God, should not be broken. This experience was therefore also a fulfillment of prophecy.

The Burial of Christ

Another Old Testament prophecy was fulfilled in the burial of Jesus: "He made His grave with the wicked, and with the rich in His death; because He had done no violence, neither was any deceit in His mouth." Isaiah 53:9. The fulfillment of this prophecy is recorded in Matthew 27:57-60.

The burial of Jesus in the tomb of a wealthy man is remarkable when we consider the fact that burial, especially in a sepulcher, was absolutely forbidden by Roman law to crucified persons. They were usually left on the cross to decay or to be devoured by dogs or wild beasts and birds of prey. "Distracted relatives and friends saw the birds of prey attack the very faces of those whom they loved; and pity often took pains to scare away the birds by day and the beasts by night, or to outwit the guards that watched the dead."—"*Jesus of Nazareth*," *Theodor Keim, vol. 6, p. 250.*

Pilate was glad to grant the request of Joseph because he knew that Jesus was innocent. He was also anxious to ease his guilty conscience. Since Jesus was not a criminal, He did not deserve the death and burial of a criminal. Pilate had several times declared Him guiltless, and he therefore either concluded that the Roman law did not apply or he did it as a rebuff to the Jews. Jesus made His grave "with the rich in His death; because He had done no violence, neither was any deceit in His mouth." From every viewpoint, the events in the life and death of Jesus prove conclusively that He was the Messiah of the Jews and the Saviour of men.

CHAPTER TWENTY-FIVE

THE POWER OF THE CROSS

THE trials and crucifixion of Jesus constituted not only the most notorious judicial blunder but also the most awful crime ever committed in the history of mankind. The whole world stands charged with the deliberate rejection and murder of the Son of God, and for this crime the human race will be called to account by the Supreme Judge of the universe. The cross is not only the means of salvation; it also stands as the symbol of injustice. "The dishonor of Golgotha is the dishonor of justice. And it has been a wise measure to remove the crucifix from almost all the halls of justice among Christian nations, since this sign frequently discredits the work of the judges." "The cross of His martyrdom will stand fixed forever upon the crowning summit of injustice, cupidity, and civil falsehood, a symbol of eternal reprobation and of regeneration without limit." —*"The Trial of Jesus," Rosadi, pages 142, 313.*

The cross of Calvary was the meeting place of the two eternities as well as the focal point of human history. On the summit of Golgotha one dispensation ended and the other began. There the gospel types met their antitypes, and the shadows converged into the substance. The death of Christ was the signal for the consummation of the figurative services in the earthly temple, or sanctuary, and the announcement that the ministration of "the sanctuary, and of the true tabernacle, which the Lord pitched, and not man," was about to begin. The Lamb of God, the true sacrificial victim, had shed His precious blood as the price of man's redemption, and could therefore go into the presence of God to make intercession for His people. The Priest of the heavenly sanctuary could now plead His own blood before the Eternal in the repentant sinner's behalf.

"Jesus, when He had cried again with a loud voice, yielded up the ghost. And, behold, the veil of the temple was rent in twain from the top to the bottom; and the earth did quake, and the rocks rent; and the graves were opened; and many bodies of the saints which slept arose, and came out of the graves after His resurrection, and went into the Holy City, and appeared unto many." Matthew 27: 50-53. Paul tells us that these resurrected saints ascended with Christ when He returned to heaven. See Ephesians 4: 8, margin. The twenty-four elders and their assistants, who are said to have been redeemed from the earth by Christ's blood and who assist Him in the heavenly sanctuary service, are those who were taken to heaven with Christ as trophies of His resurrection victory; they are the first fruits of the great gospel harvest of redeemed souls.

Jesus died at the very hour of the evening sacrifice, when the paschal lamb, representing Him, was ready to be slain by the officiating priests of the temple. "Clothed in his significant and beautiful dress, the priest stood with lifted knife, as did Abraham when he was about to slay his son. With intense interest the people were looking on. But the earth trembles and quakes; for the Lord Himself draws near. With a rending noise the inner veil of the temple is torn from top to bottom by an unseen hand, throwing open to the gaze of the multitude a place once filled with the presence of God. In this place the Shekinah had dwelt. Here God had manifested His glory above the mercy seat. No one but the high priest ever lifted the veil separating this apartment from the rest of the temple. He entered in once a year to make an atonement for the sins of the people. But lo, this veil is rent in twain. The most holy place of the earthly sanctuary is no longer sacred. . . . Type has met antitype in the death of God's Son. The great sacrifice has been made. The way into the holiest is laid open. A new and living way is prepared for all."—"*The Desire of Ages,*" *pages 756, 757.*

The Far-Reaching Consequences of Calvary

The plan of redemption centers in the cross of Calvary, and therefore could not be fully comprehended until after that event. The apostle Paul declared that "the mystery" of redemption, which he calls "the unsearchable riches of Christ," "from the beginning of the world hath been hid in God, who created all things by Jesus Christ: to the intent that now unto the principalities and powers in heavenly places might be known by the church the manifold wisdom of God, according to the eternal purpose which He purposed in Christ Jesus our Lord." Ephesians 3: 8-11. The cross alone could bring to man and to the universe "the revelation of the mystery, which was kept secret since the world began." Romans 16: 25.

The death cry of Jesus, "It is finished," meant far more than the announcement of the completion of the typical service, the fulfillment of the Messianic prophecies, and the consummation of the plan of salvation that saves man and his lost dominion. It also embraced the death knell of Satan's revolt, and the reconciliation of the entire universe to God. The unexplainable "mystery of iniquity" had left an unanswered question in the minds of angels and unfallen beings, which was equivalent to a partial alienation from God. This question was fully and finally answered by the cross, by which, therefore, a permanent reconciliation was effected. The mystery of the cross explains all other mysteries. Just before the crisis of Gethsemane and Calvary, Jesus said: "Now is the judgment of this world: now shall the prince of this world be cast out. And I, if I be lifted up from the earth, will draw all men unto Me. This He said, signifying what death He should die." John 12: 31-33.

The word "men" is in italics, indicating that it was supplied by the translators. That the "all" includes far more than the inhabitants of this rebel world is indicated by another text: "It pleased the Father that in Him should all fullness dwell; and, having made peace through the blood of His cross, by Him to reconcile all things unto Himself; by Him, I say, whether they be things in earth, or things in heaven. And you, that were sometime alienated and enemies in your mind by wicked works, yet now hath He reconciled in the body of His flesh through death, to present you holy and unblamable and unreprovable in His sight." Colossians 1: 19-22. The death of Christ on the cross reconciled the whole universe to God, including "things in heaven" as well as "things in earth."

The incarnation and the atoning death of Christ make possible the final destruction of Satan and all his followers: "Forasmuch then as the children are partakers of flesh and blood, He also Himself likewise took part of the same; that through death He might destroy him that had the power of death, that is, the devil; and deliver them who through fear of death were all their lifetime subject to bondage." Hebrews 2: 14, 15. As far as the sinless angels and unfallen beings were concerned, Satan and His angels could have been destroyed at any time after Jesus died on the cross, because every question had been answered and every vestige of sympathy destroyed. The entire universe had witnessed the scenes of Calvary, where they saw the final unveiling of "the mystery of iniquity" and the completed revelation of the character of the great rebel. The decisive battle had been fought; Satan had suffered a crushing defeat, and knew that his cause and kingdom were lost.

It Takes Time

The execution of the archapostate and his followers must be delayed until the gospel message has time to bring the inhabitants of the earth to a final decision as to whom they will serve and to which of the two rival governments they will give their allegiance. When the gospel has completed its mission, and probation closes, the execution of sinners can take place with the approval of the entire universe. One writer says: "By the facts unfolded in the progress of the great controversy, God will demonstrate the principles of His rules of government, which have been falsified by Satan and by all whom he has deceived. His justice will finally be acknowledged by the whole world, though the acknowledgment will be too late to save the rebellious. God carries with Him the sympathy and approval of the whole universe as step by step His great plan advances to its complete fulfillment."—"*Patriarchs and Prophets*," *page 79.* It is for this reason that when Satan and sinners are finally destroyed their execution will meet with such general approval that "affliction shall not rise up the second time." Nahum 1:9. It takes time permanently to cure the disease of sin and to remove all its effects from the universe so that it cannot again lift its ugly head to plague the sons of God. Like all successful operations, there must of necessity be much pain and suffering before there can be a permanent cure.

As the cry from the cross, "It is finished," echoed throughout the universe, it was recognized not as an admission of defeat but as a shout of victory over Satan. The prophet John records the celestial note of triumph in Revelation 12: 10-13: "I heard a loud voice saying in heaven, Now is come salvation, and strength, and the kingdom of our God, and the power of His Christ: for the accuser of our brethren is cast down, which accused them before our God day and night. And they overcame him by the blood of the Lamb, and by the word of their testimony; and they loved not their lives unto the death. Therefore rejoice, ye heavens, and ye that dwell in them. Woe to the inhabiters of the earth and of the sea! for the devil is come down unto you, having great wrath, because he knoweth that he hath but a short time. And when the dragon saw that he was cast unto the earth, he persecuted the woman which brought forth the man child."

The devil never knew that his cause was lost and that his time was short until Jesus died a conqueror on the cross of Calvary. This was the event that withdrew from him all sympathy and divested him of his position as "the prince of this world." He was then cast out as this world's usurper, prince, and ruler, and Jesus became the world's true prince and representative in the councils of heaven. The cross was the weapon that sealed the doom of the great rebel leader, who knows that it is only a question of time until he shall be stripped of all authority and power and shall be imprisoned in the bottomless pit to await a just sentence at the close of the millennium.

The cross is the greatest of all evidences of the love of God. After the death of a certain prisoner, there was found on the wall of his cell a picture of a large cross with the word "Love" written at the four ends of the two beams, indicating that the cross alone measures the height, depth, and breadth of the love of God "which passeth knowledge." While the highway of holiness is sprinkled with blood, it is also paved with love. The cross is the science of salvation, and it will be the song of the redeemed throughout all eternity. E. G. White writes: "To remove the cross from the Christian would be like blotting the sun from the sky. The cross brings us near to God, reconciling us to Him. . . . Without the cross, man could have no union with the Father. On it depends our every hope. From it shines the light of the Saviour's love; and when at the foot of the cross the sinner looks up to the One who died to save him, he may rejoice with fullness of joy; for his sins are pardoned. Kneeling in faith at the cross, he has reached the highest place to which man can attain."—*"The Acts of the Apostles," pages 209, 210.*

It is the thought of Calvary that awakens sacred and living emotions in our hearts. It is impossible for pride and selfishness to flourish in the heart that keeps fresh in memory the scenes of Calvary. The reflections of the love of God as demonstrated by the cross will renovate the mind, touch and melt the soul, refine and elevate the affections, and completely transform the whole character. No wonder the apostle Paul cried out, enraptured by his vision of the cross: "God forbid that I should glory, save in the cross of our Lord Jesus Christ, by whom the world is crucified unto me, and I unto the world." Galatians 6: 14.

May God give us all the same glorious vision and living experience.

BIBLIOGRAPHY

Besides the Authorized, the American Standard, and other versions of the Scriptures used as the chief source of information in this volume, the following books have directly and indirectly furnished material aid:

BENNY, PHILIP BERGER, *The Criminal Code of the Jews.* Smith, Elder & Company, London, 1880.

BIRKENHEAD, THE EARL OF, *Famous Trials of History.* Garden City Publishing Co., Inc., Garden City, New York, 1926.

BLACKSTONE, SIR WILLIAM. Edited and annotated by Thomas M. Cooley. Callaghan and Company, Chicago, 1884.

CAMBRIDGE BIBLE, THE. University Press, Cambridge, England, 1893-1910.

CHANDLER, WALTER M., of the New York bar, *The Trial of Jesus,* 2 vols. The Federal Book Co., New York, 1925.

CICERO, M. TULLII, *Orations.* Whittaker and Company, London, 1896.

COLLETT, SIDNEY, *Scripture of Truth.*

CREVIER, J. B. L., *History of the Roman Emperors.*

DEUTSCH, EMANUEL, *The Talmud.* The Jewish Publication Society of America, Philadelphia, 1896.

DION CASSIUS.

DUPIN, M., French advocate and doctor of laws, *The Trial of Jesus Before Caiaphas and Pilate.* Translated into English by John Pickering, LL. D., Counselor-at-law and President of the American Academy of Arts and Sciences.

EDERSHEIM, ALFRED, *The Life and Times of Jesus the Messiah.* Longmans, Green, and Company, New York, 1906.

ELLICOTT, DR. CHARLES J., *Historical Lectures on the Life of Our Lord Jesus Christ.*

GEIKIE, CUNNINGHAM, *The Life and Words of Christ.* John B. Alden, New York, 1885.

GIBBON, EDWARD, *The History of the Decline and Fall of the Roman Empire.* With notes by Rev. H. H. Milman. Porter & Coates, Philadelphia.

GREENLEAF, SIMON, LL. D., professor of law in Harvard University, *The Testimony of the Evangelists Examined by the Rules of Evidence Administered in Courts of Justice.* Soney & Sage, Newark, New Jersey, 1903.

GREENIDGE, A. H. J., *The Legal Procedure of Cicero's Time*. Stevens & Sons, London, 1901.

INNES, A. TAYLOR, Lawyer, *The Trial of Jesus Christ*. T. and T. Clark, Edinburgh, 1905.

JOSEPHUS, FLAVIUS, Jewish historian, *Antiquities of the Jews*. Whiston's translation.

KEIM, T[illegible]DOR, *Jesus of Nazareth*, 6 vols. Williams & Norgate, Lo[illegible] [illegible].

LEMANN, MM., *Jesus Before the Sanhedrin*. Translated into English by Prof. Julius Magath of Oxford, Georgia, 1899.

LIVY, TITUS, *The History of Rome*. George Bell & Sons, London, 1906.

MENDELSOHN, *Hebrew Maxims and Rules*.

MENDELSOHN, S., *The Criminal Jurisprudence of the Ancient Hebrews*. M. Curlander, Baltimore, 1891.

MILLINGEN, J. G., M. D., *Curiosities of Medical Experience*.

MISHNA, THE. Edition of Surenhusius, Amsterdam, 1698-1703.

PALEY, WILLIAM, *Evidences of Christianity*. The Religious Tract Society, London, 1794.

PLUTARCH.

RENAN, ERNEST, *The Life of Jesus*. A. L. Burt Company, New York.

ROBERTSON, ARCHIBALD THOMAS, *Word Pictures in the New Testament*. Richard R. Smith, Inc., New York, 1930.

ROSADI, GIOVANNI, Italian advocate, *The Trial of Jesus*. Dodds, Mead and Company, New York, 1905.

RUSSELL, DR. DAVID, *Letters, Chiefly Practical and Consolatory*.

SALVADOR, JOSEPH, Jewish physician and scholar, *Histoire des Institutions de Moise*. Michel Levy-Freres, Paris, 1862.

SCHAFF, PHILIP, *The Person of Christ*.

STARKIE on Evidence.

STROUD, WILLIAM, M. D., *The Physical Cause of the Death of Christ*. Hamilton, Adams & Co., London, 1871.

SUETONIUS TRANQUILLUS, *The Lives of the Twelve Caesars*. George Bell & Sons, London, 1906.

TACITUS, *The Works of Tacitus*. American Book Company, New York, 1904.

TALMUD, THE, Babylonian Recension. Translated into English by Michael L. Rodkinson, New Talmud Publishing Company, New York, 1896.

WHITE, MRS. E. G., *The Desire of Ages*. Pacific Press Publishing Association, Mountain View, California, 1898.

WISE, ISAAC M., Jewish Rabbi, *The Martyrdom of Jesus*. The Bloch Publishing and Printing Company, Cincinnati and Chicago, 1888.